THE ONLY BUSINESS C⊕MPASS YOU WILL EVER NEED

THE NORTHSTAR STRATEGIC PARTNERS
4 POINTS OF FOCUS™

Wendy Roberts

Copyright © 2024 NorthStar Strategic Partners, Inc.

All rights reserved. It is not legal to reproduce, duplicate or transmit any part of this document in either electronic means or printed format. Recording of this publication is strictly prohibited without written permission.

Disclaimer

This book contains references to fictional businesses and their owners. Any resemblance to actual businesses, living or deceased, or to real individuals, is purely coincidental. The names, characters, businesses, places, and incidents are the product of the author's imagination or are used fictitiously. The author does not intend to endorse or defame any real businesses or individuals. Any similarities to real businesses or persons, living or deceased, are entirely unintentional.

Publisher: Chestnut Publishing House, LLC | www.chestnutbooks.com

Editor: Ruth Fae - Fae Blood Publications | www.faebloodpublications.com.au

Book Designer: Kristina Conatser | www.capturedbykcdesigns.com

ISBN: 979-8-218-35371-1

DEDICATED TO:

All the business owners who are struggling to figure out how to grow a profitable and sustainable business that will give you the greatest value when you are ready to exit,

AND

Our resolute staff and awesome customers for the continued support and confidence to create the magic,

AND finally,

To my Dad who gave me the entrepreneurial spirit,
To my Mom who said you can do anything in life,
as long as you put your mind to it,
To my spouse, family, friends, and mentors,
thank you for all the love and support to
make this book a reality!

TABLE OF CONTENTS

Introduction 7

    Profitability 10

    Scalability 12

    Sustainability 13

    Creating an Organization of Value 14

    NorthStar and the 4 Points of Focus 16

Section 1: Marketing Strategies, the Red Point of Focus 19

    The Marketing Strategy: Creating an Effective Plan 20

    The Marketing Budget 25

    Measure Your Results 26

    What is a "Target Market" and How do You Define Yours? 27

    Branding 28

    Defining Your Value Proposition 30

    Pricing Strategy 32

    Promotional Marketing Assets and Their Impact on the Endgame 33

    What Experts Say About Marketing Strategies as a Point of Focus 34

Section 2: Financial Structure & Growth, the Green Point of Focus 35

    Why Financial Structure & Growth are Important for a Healthy Business 35

    Understanding the Different Legal Financial Structures for Your Business 36

    Why You Need a Solid Financial System as the Foundation of Your Business ... 39

    How to Use Your Financial Statements to Tell the Story of Your Business 41

    What an Income Statement is and What it Tells You 42

    How Your Balance Sheet Helps You Understand Your Assets, Liabilities, and Equity 43

    Using Your Cash Flow Statement in a Cash Management Best Practice 44

    Profit 45

Key Tips for Your Business to Manage Growth and Maintain Stability Through Your Financial Structure & Growth Point of Focus 47

What Experts Say About the Financial Structure & Growth Point of Focus 49

Section 3: Operational Excellence, the Orange Point of Focus.............................. 51

Being Strategic 53

Set Your Key Performance Indicators (KPIs) 55

Creating Operational Processes and Systems for Optimal Performance and Efficiency 56

Managing Your Operational Performance..60

Leading Your Company Tone in a Culture of Continuous Improvement 62

Effectively Document Operational Systems and Processes....................63

How to Establish a Documentation Process...65

Implementing the Documentation Procedure.......................................66

Best Practices for Updating Your Documentation 67

What Experts Say About Operational Excellence and Continuous Improvement 69

Section 4: People & Team Building, the Blue Point of Focus.................................. 71

People Relationship Dynamics in a Company 72

How Does Your Company Stack Up? 72

How Leadership Can Build Trust and Rapport..73

The Ten Most Important Qualities of a High-Functioning Business Team..........73

Communication Strategies to Bolster Employee Interaction 75

The Interpersonal Relationships in Your Company 75

How to Make "Personality" Work for Your Company.............................77

How to Identify "Who's Who in the Zoo?"..79

How to Praise Your Employees 81

How to Reprimand Your Employees 83

Motivational Strategies to Use to Attract Great Team Members and Retain Them..85

What Experts Say About the Value of Your People to Your Organization... 87

Explorer Jack and His Distribution Company 88

Section 5: The North Star, Polaris, and the Exit Strategy 89

Your Marketing Strategies Value 90

Your Financial Structure & Growth Value 91

Your Operational Excellence Value 92

Your People & Team Building Value 94

Valuation Methods to Determine the Worth of Your Company
and When to Sell It 95

Understanding the Different Types of Buyers 96

Putting Together Your Business Sales Team and Process 97

What Experts Say About Exit Strategies 99

Epilogue 101

What are Your Next Steps? 104

About the Author 105

Acknowledgements 106

References 107

INTRODUCTION

A business leader can be like a lost explorer...

Jack was an adventurous explorer who loved to travel to remote places and discover new things. Leading his team of people, he explored the Amazon rainforest, Sahara Desert, Himalayas, and many other exotic locations. Jack always carried his own tools and essential items in his backpack: a knife, flashlight, water bottle, and a compass that someone advised him might be useful.

One day, he and his group decided to explore a dense jungle in Africa. Having heard rumors of a hidden temple that contained ancient treasures and secrets, he made finding the temple his group's mission. Jack hired a local guide to take his team and him to the edge of the jungle, then he and the group ventured alone into the green wilderness.

They walked for hours, following a faint trail that Jack hoped would lead them to the temple. Along the way, he saw many strange and beautiful plants and animals. Fascinated by his surroundings, and feeling like he was in another world, he didn't notice how far they had gone or how dark it had become. But, as luck would have it, he and his team stumbled upon the temple, where they gained great knowledge and expertise. They meticulously documented their find with valuable photography, videos, and commentary, sure they would garner a fortune upon their return to civilization. But they did not know how they got there, and they did not know where to go next. They had no exit strategy!

Jack realized this mistake when he tried to retrace his steps. No one could find the trail anymore. They were lost. Jack panicked and ran in different directions, hoping to find a way out, but he only led the team deeper into the jungle. They started to hear strange noises, and felt as though eyes were watching them from the shadows. Were they being hunted?

Thankfully, Jack remembered his compass. He took it out of his backpack, looked at it, and saw it pointed north. Hoping it would lead the team to safety and knowing that north of the jungle was a river that flowed towards a village, he decided to follow it; if they could reach the river, they could find help.

Looking up at the night sky, Jack saw a bright star—the North Star—shining above him. He knew that it always stayed in the same position in the sky and aligned with the north pole of the Earth. Knowing it would work in conjunction with his compass, he felt more confident and reassured.

He and his team walked north for what seemed like an eternity. They had to overcome many obstacles and dangers along the way, climbing over fallen trees, crossing muddy swamps, avoiding poisonous snakes and spiders, and dodging hungry lions and leopards. They were exhausted, thirsty, hungry, and scared. But Jack didn't give up. He kept following his compass and the North Star, trusting them to guide him out of the jungle. He knew they were their only hope.

Finally, after many hours of walking, they saw a glimmer of light in the distance. The team ran towards it, hoping it was the river. Jack was right! When they reached the river, they saw some fishermen on a boat. Jack waved and shouted for help, so the fishermen came to their rescue, giving them water, food, and a ride to the village.

Jack and his team were safe. They had their benefits from the temple and had escaped the jungle. Relieved, and filled with gratitude, Jack thanked his rescuers, his compass, and the North Star. As a leader, he realized he had been very lucky, as well as foolish, but this experience taught him what his true resources were, and he decided to be more careful and prepared in his future adventures.

He learned a valuable lesson: focus on your North Star and set your compass around it accordingly. While your journey may have some successes, failures can ruin you. Only your North Star can guide you through your success, to your exit strategy, to your ultimate win!

Focus is the Key to Success in Business.

It is not about doing more things but doing the *right* things. It is not about being busy but being productive. It is not about being distracted but being persistent.

Your business can bring you "the wealth of the temple" if you guide yourself and your team effectively toward your goals and objectives. But achieving those goals is only half the story; the true secret to your success lies in keeping your profitability sustained—and increasing—as you reach your end game or exit strategy.

You are not done until you're done. Your exit may be to sell the business, sell your share in the business, or to plan a transition to your heir apparent.

This Book, and Our Guidance, is Your North Star.

This book is like Jack's compass. Here, we introduce you to the *4 Points of Focus*, and like a magnetically-balanced direction system, these Points will guide you to success and profitability, and give you an ongoing framework on which to build your business.

NorthStar Strategic Partners are the developers of the *4 Points of Focus* concept. NorthStar prides itself on partnering with open-minded, growth-oriented businesses who are willing to make a change. In starting this journey, the company had one common goal in mind: to be the glue that helps hold companies together and succeed. Business owners can be so close to their operation that it can be difficult to step back and see what needs to be tweaked, adjusted, and maneuvered to lead to the best outcomes. This is exactly where NorthStar comes in to help. It is the goal post to achieving your ultimate victory, and acts as your guide in using your 4 Points of Focus compass.

NorthStar will ask the questions that you may not think to ask and examine the issues that may not always be surface level. Whether a business owner is struggling to achieve growth, retain employees, or simply make a profit, NorthStar is always ready and willing to offer advice through expert business consulting.

This book holds the principles that we infuse into your business practices to coach and support you.

NorthStar is My Brainchild.

I am Wendy Roberts, CEO of NorthStar Strategic Partners. My first move in this role was to envision our mission and principles.

The first thing I like to tell people is that I am left-handed. Why is this important? Because I will always approach things with out-of-box, solution-oriented, non-cookie-cutter innovation. I lead our company that way, and I will influence yours that way as well. I have a vast record of driving powerful strategies using emerging technologies including data analytics, artificial intelligence, cybersecurity, and governance, risk and compliance solutions.

As an accomplished Global Finance Executive, Audit Committee member, and Business Advisor, I have over twenty-five-years in financial and audit leadership, operations expertise, and technology innovation experience for both SMB (small and midsize businesses) and multinational companies. As a Corporate Finance executive, I delivered relevant expertise in Corporate Strategy, Risk Management, Financial Reporting, Merger and Acquisition, IT Operations, Audit/SOX reporting and system implementations. I have functioned as the CFO for various startups, including successfully selling an early-stage software company to a large publicly traded company. I spent many years in the public accounting area, delivering solid results for my customers in Accounting, Audit, Tax, and IT systems.

CPA licensed, I have also held the CIA, CISA and CCSA designations and MCSE in IT systems engineering. I am currently serving on the Audit

Committee of The Tech Interactive, a world leader in the creation of immersive STEAM education resources to develop the next generation of problem solvers.

With our *4 Points of Focus* as your compass, you can take your business to an optimal level of profitability, scalability, sustainability, and ultimately achieve an organization of value, whether you choose to open it to acquisition or other end-game options. When you address and document your strategy around the *NorthStar Strategic Partners 4 Points of Focus*, you have a complete overall business plan.

PROFITABILITY

What exactly is "profitability?" Profit truly is an essential metric that indicates the success of a business and represents the revenue generated after all expenses are deducted.

Small businesses frequently talk about being in pursuit of profitability. To achieve this, small businesses must follow some necessary principles that are crucial to your success, and that we have encapsulated into the *4 Points of Focus*. Through these *4 Points*, small businesses can take a disciplined approach towards your business management. This includes:

- Maintaining accurate records of your transactions
- Tracking your expenses and income
- Regularly comparing your financial performance against your targets

The *4 Points* will enable businesses to understand your financial health and improve your decision-making processes. In following this process, small businesses will learn to be intentional when incurring costs. You should only spend money on acquiring assets or services that add value to your business. Overhead costs, such as rent, utilities, and salaries, should be kept at a level that is additive to the health of the business.

Pricing

The Pricing Strategy for the business should be optimized to ensure it aligns with the market demand, while also covering costs and generating profits.

Small businesses should not rush into discounting your products or services, as this could result in reduced revenue and profitability. The Pricing Strategy should be based on the value offered rather than only the cost of production. Businesses can add value by offering unique features, exceptional customer service, and convenient payment options.

Cash Flow Management

The *4 Points of Focus* also embrace Cash Flow Management. Small businesses need to manage their cash flow effectively to prevent running out of funds, which could lead to bankruptcy.

This involves monitoring cash inflows and outflows, forecasting future cash requirements, and ensuring that invoices are paid on time. Businesses can negotiate better payment terms with suppliers or request a down payment or deposit to boost your cash position. Good Cash Flow Management enables businesses to:

- Pay bills on time
- Avoid late fees
- Manage debts
- Invest in growth opportunities

Marketing

Our *4 Points of Focus* inspire small businesses to invest in marketing to reach out to potential customers. Effective marketing can attract new customers, increase revenue, and improve the brand's visibility.

A marketing initiative should also include the efforts small businesses need to apply to retain loyal customers who frequently avail their services. Long-term customers provide a steady source of income and can help to build positive recommendations and repeat business.

A small business will improve profitability by implementing effective sales and marketing efforts. This involves:

- Identifying and reaching your target market
- Building relationships with your customers
- Promoting your products or services

Utilizing cost-effective marketing methods such as social media, email marketing, and referrals can help you reach more customers without incurring high marketing costs. With these sales and marketing activities, your business can increase your revenue, which ultimately boosts your profitability.

Operations

The *4 Points* compass contains guidance for small businesses to constantly strive to improve your operations. This can include adopting new technology, exploring alternative suppliers, and automating redundant and time-consuming tasks.

Good Operational Efficiency for the business will be careful not to compromise the quality of its products or services, as customers are willing to pay more when they receive value for their money. Effective operations will also impact your cost control. Small businesses need to keep operating costs low without jeopardizing the quality of your products or services. By reducing expenses, small companies can increase your profit margins, which boosts your overall profitability.

You will find that the *4 Points of Focus do require discipline, hard work, and patience. But when implemented correc*tly, they will make your small businesses profitable and pave the way for growth.

SCALABILITY

The *4 Points of Focus* give a small business or entrepreneurship "scalability." This is the ability to adapt and change in size and scope to capitalize on opportunities and keep the business healthy in times when there is a need to scale back.

Achieving scalability may seem like a daunting task for small businesses, but it is essential for growth and success. The *4 Points of Focus* guide businesses in scalability by directing you to identify your core competencies and find ways to optimize them. Scalability relies on creating efficient processes that can be replicated as the business grows. This will not only increase productivity, but also reduce costs.

Another crucial aspect of scalability is investing in technology and automation, which can streamline the operations and allow the business to handle more volume without the need for additional staff. Additionally, outsourcing non-core activities can free up resources and allow you to focus on growth opportunities.

Scalability is one of the most sought-after goals for a small business trying to grow fast and generate more revenue. It means being able to increase output, revenue, and profits quickly, as demand grows, without being hindered by a lack of resources or ability to keep up. To achieve scalability, small businesses must build a solid foundation of systems and processes that can be scaled up as needed. This includes everything from the way you organize your work to the way you deliver services or products. It also means investing in technology that can automate many aspects of the business, thus reducing the amount of time and resources required to achieve growth goals.

Leadership

Having a strong and adaptable leadership team is key. Encouraging employees to think creatively and explore new opportunities can help to drive innovation and growth.

It is vital, therefore, to have the right team in place, comprised of people who are skilled, dedicated, and willing to go the extra mile to get the job done. This includes both full-time employees as well as freelancers or contract workers who can fill in the gaps as needed. The team must be aligned around the company's goals and vision and be able to work together effectively to achieve them. This often requires investing in training and development programs to help team members build their skills and stay on top of industry best practices.

Marketing and Branding

Marketing and Branding are also crucial to achieving scalability. Small businesses need to create a strong and evolving brand identity that resonates with your target audience, and develop marketing campaigns that engage people and encourage them to become customers.

This requires a deep understanding of:
- Who your customer is
- What they value now, and will value in the future
- How they want, and will want, to be approached

It also means continuously creating compelling content that attracts attention and builds trust.

Innovation

A relentless focus on innovation and continuous improvement is essential for small businesses trying to achieve scalability. This involves constantly testing new ideas, being willing to pivot when things are not working, and staying ahead of trends and changes in the industry. It also means learning from failures and iterating quickly to improve processes and products.

Small businesses will be well-positioned to achieve your growth goals if you are willing to:

- Build a strong and flexible foundation of systems and processes
- Invest in technology
- Build a talented team
- Develop strong branding and marketing campaigns
- Focus on continuous innovation and improvement

SUSTAINABILITY

As a crucial issue for small businesses to reach your ultimate value and attract acquisition, sustainability encompasses a broad range of considerations. At the core of sustainability is the idea of balancing economic, environmental, and social factors, which requires a coordinated effort across all aspects of your business.

Marketing: The focus area of Marketing is a critical element of sustainability, as it can shape how a small business is perceived and trusted in the marketplace, and influence its customer base.

Financial Systems: The focus area of Financial Systems must be carefully managed to ensure the long-term financial health of your business.

Operations: Operational Excellence is also essential, as it can reduce costs and increase efficiency, ultimately contributing to your business' overall sustainability.

People & Team Building: People & Team Building is yet another area of critical importance, as attracting and retaining talented employees is a key factor in small business sustainability.

By fostering a supportive and engaging work environment, small businesses can build a strong team of skilled individuals who are committed to the success of your organization. In addition, retention and attraction of talent can be influenced by offering training and development opportunities, promoting work-life balance, and providing competitive benefits packages.

Small businesses that prioritize sustainability will be best positioned to thrive in the long-term and prepare the company for its next step of trajectory—attracting loyal customers and talented employees while enjoying financial stability and operational efficiency.

CREATING AN ORGANIZATION OF VALUE

Ultimately, you want to create a business that is valuable. In his book, *How to Grow Your Small Business*, Donald Miller points out qualities that help reinforce your value. Rather than trying to be everything to everyone, look to your strengths and what you do best. Be willing to change as your business landscape changes. Relationships are key. These include your relationships with your customers, partners, and employees. Trust and rapport are your superpowers. Give back to your community.

Like most things in life, businesses have a beginning, a middle, and an end. This is a reality many small business owners do not envision when they launch their company. They start the company with a vague notion that they, and it, will continue forever.

While the goal of sustainability might fortify that notion, it is ultimately both unrealistic and ill advised. The company will serve you best when you have an endgame concept. Where do you want to be after you release the company? How you release it may be to end it, or to bequeath it to heirs, or to sell it. The latter is the most powerful and recommended.

Get an exit strategy that includes you creating a company of value that a third party will want to buy from you. As John Warrillow, author of *Built to Sell* points out, "The best businesses are built to sell. They're designed to be easy to understand, operate, and transfer to a new owner."

Your Roadmap to Success

Create capital for yourself and your next great adventure. The plan should outline the best times and ways for the owner to divest of the company, taking into account market conditions, economic and legal factors, and potential tax implications. A well-thought-out exit strategy can help the owners lay out a roadmap for success, enabling them to maximize their return on investment and minimize risks.

Creating a business of value for acquisition requires a comprehensive understanding of what buyers look for when purchasing a company:

<u>Your People:</u> Buyers are interested in acquiring businesses that possess seasoned employees with specialized skills, and a culture of corporate professionalism that can be sustained after the acquisition.

<u>Your Systems:</u> The value of a system or process that empowers your staff to perform efficiently cannot be overstated. A system that captures your company's unique practices and processes is a key factor that attracts buyers.

<u>Your Financial Health:</u> Your company's financial health, including cash flow, financial statements, and debt levels, should be up-to-date, and financial projections should also be available.

<u>Your Branding:</u> The value of a recognized brand cannot be overemphasized. A company that has successfully established market recognition is a valuable asset whose market worth may even exceed the value of its tangible assets.

To create a business of value for acquisition, every small business owner needs to have a plan. The *4 Points of Focus* lays down the steps to:

- Create a business
- Identify market niches
- Outline key milestones
- Develop strategies for growth

By using the well-documented plan the *4 Points of Focus* delivers, it becomes easier for owners to identify systems and employees that are valuable to the company, and address any deficiencies.

Creating a business of value for acquisition is not an easy task. A small business owner must understand what buyers desire when seeking acquisition opportunities, have a solid plan in place—with an emphasis on systems, employees, and a recognized brand—and have an exit strategy. This is the ultimate goal of the *4 Points of Focus*. It is the true "North Star," the destination to which you can head.

Following the best practices of the *4 Points of Focus* can provide the foundation for a successful acquisition and transition of ownership.

NORTHSTAR AND THE 4 POINTS OF FOCUS

NorthStar Strategic Partners are business consultants who can guide you to your North Star of success, excellence, and valuable profits. In our process, as we define throughout this book, you determine exactly what your personal Polaris will be for you and your company.

What are your ideals, your goals, and the dream you wish to achieve?

By answering that question, we create a bright and steady guiding light your whole team can see looking forward. As you utilize the *4 Points of Focus*, your business will travel on its true north path. The proven methodology will help you exceed your objectives and supersize your company's value.

Within the *4 Points of Focus*, we have identified the crucial aspects of your business. Should you perform to even 80% of your potential in all these areas, you will surpass your highest revenue ideals, keep a generous portion of your profits, achieve your wildest dreams, and make your company a highly desired acquisition when you decide to make a lucrative exit.

Here is Your Magic Formula:

Your Percentage of Achievement in Marketing

x

Your Percentage of Achievement in Finance

x

Your Percentage of Achievement in Operations

x

Your Percentage of Achievement in People & Team Building

=

Your Level of Success

Here are the values of the *4 Points of Focus*:

Red - Marketing: bullseye, luck, passion. We guide you to generate revenue with the right marketing investments, to capture a loyal customer base, and to earn high business return for your marketing expenditures.

Once captured, we help you with the adhesiveness needed to achieve lifetime business from your hard-earned customers.

Green - Finance: money, richness, bountiful. We show you financial systems that maximize your revenue. We analyze your profit margin—your gross profit, working capital, and net profit—and work with you on your strategy to make each the most it can be.

Orange - Operations: innovation, try something different, out of your comfort zone. We guide you to reduce and remove waste that detracts from your revenue profits. After identifying your ideal net profit and perfecting the stream of working capital, these must be protected by sound and efficient operations that are both cost-saving and mission-effective. They must integrate factors from system agility to cost accuracy with the lowest financial outlay possible.

Elevate your assets while minimizing your liabilities. Your operations must be documented and executable by anyone stepping into place; procedures cannot only exist in the mind and behavior of an individual employee.

Blue - People: trust, true blue, depth of the ocean. We show you how to develop and retain talent that makes your company valuable, and strengthen your team and its combined abilities. We take you through our NorthStar proprietary gap analysis to assess your existing team, their level of job ability, and their satisfaction compared to highly effective company teams in your industry.

This book will help you find your North Star.

65% of businesses fail in their first decade. Do not be an industry statistic.

Go for your North Star, the Polaris, that will set the direction of your company. Working together, we can develop the strategic actions that will take you there.

When you read this book and work with us, you will receive practical advice and guidance as well as a full repertoire of tools to transform your business. No matter the enterprise, from financial analysis to operational systems, from optimizing your team to marketing strategies, we provide strategic business planning and execution services customized to help your company succeed.

SECTION 1: MARKETING STRATEGIES, THE RED POINT OF FOCUS

The first of the *4 Points of Focus* is Marketing Strategies, it is Red for the passion it exudes for, and within, your company.

As virtual business mentor, Michael Hyatt, has stated, "Marketing is really just about sharing your passion." Red is the color of passion, and passion certainly is the heart of marketing. Often, when we dig into the concept of Marketing Strategies, that passion becomes a rather complex endeavor.

"Marketing" is a broad term that encompasses many activities related to the promoting and selling of products or services to customers, partners, and society at large. It involves:

- Research, creation, communication, delivery, and exchange of offerings that have value for the target market

- Analysis and understanding of the needs, wants, preferences, and behaviors of customers and potential customers

- Creation and maintenance of relationships with customers and other stakeholders by providing them with satisfying solutions that meet their expectations and goals

Types of Marketing

Marketing methods can be divided into two main types: inbound marketing and outbound marketing.

Inbound marketing occurs when customers initiate contact with the marketer in response to various methods used to gain their attention—email, events, content, and web design.

Outbound marketing is when the marketer initiates contact with the customer through methods such as TV, radio, and digital display advertising. Outbound marketing is often used to influence consumer awareness and preference for a brand. Marketing can also be classified into different functions or tactics, such as:

- Product marketing
- Service marketing
- Digital marketing
- Social Media marketing
- Content marketing
- Email marketing
- Event marketing
- Influencer marketing
- Affiliate marketing
- Cause marketing

Each of these functions or tactics has its own objectives, strategies, tools, and metrics to measure the effectiveness of marketing activities.

Marketing is an essential function of any small business that wants to reach and serve its customers effectively. A successful plan helps to create value for both the customers and the marketers by facilitating the exchange of goods and services that satisfy both parties' needs and wants.

THE MARKETING STRATEGY: CREATING AN EFFECTIVE PLAN

"A goal without a plan is just a wish."
—Antoine de Saint-Exupéry

"It does not do to leave a live dragon out of your calculations, if you live near him."
—J.R.R. Tolkien

The Marketing Strategy is a plan of action designed to promote and sell a product or service. It contains the company's value proposition, key brand messaging, data on target customer demographics, and other high-level elements. It is important because it provides a long-term vision for overall marketing efforts, often looking many years ahead. It helps a business achieve and communicate a sustainable competitive advantage over rival companies by understanding the needs and wants of its consumers. Your Marketing Strategy also guides the creation of more specific marketing plans which describe the concrete actions and tactics required to achieve the marketing objectives.

Remember Jack, our jungle explorer? Let's continue his story. Jack moved back to his native Ohio after his success in the jungle, and there, decided to start his own trucking and distribution service. Just as we followed Jack through his jungle adventures using his compass and the North Star, we will see how he does with his *4 Points of Focus* compass and NorthStar principles.

Jack took his adventurer wealth and bought a company called McKinley Family Logistics, a family-owned trucking and distribution company based in Geneva, Ohio. Founded in 1980 by John and Mary McKinley, the company was started with one truck and a small warehouse. Today, the McKinley Family Logistics Company has a fleet of forty trucks and a 100,000 square foot distribution center that serves customers across Ohio and neighboring states, specializing in delivering beverages to grocery stores, restaurants, and retail outlets. The company prides itself on its efficiency and has grown to an annual revenue of four million dollars, employing sixty-five people, including drivers, warehouse workers, dispatchers, and office staff.

When Jack bought the company, he had to develop his Marketing Strategy as part of his first step in the *4 Points of Focus*.

The company had previously grown organically, with no rhyme or reason. From his jungle experience, Jack knew that was not an option. So, he developed a mission and a resulting plan so he could look for key areas of opportunity.

Create Your Mission Statement

First up for Jack was defining his mission, and to be able to effectively communicate that to the organization he led, he needed to develop the Mission Statement.

The Mission Statement is a formal summary of the aims and values of a company, organization, or individual. It is used by the company to explain, in simple and concise terms, its purpose for being. The statement is generally short, either a single sentence or a short paragraph.

A Mission Statement defines a company's culture, values, ethics, fundamental goals, and agenda. It defines how each of these applies to the company's stakeholders—its employees, distributors, suppliers, shareholders, and the community at large. The ideal Mission Statement should be concise, clear, and consistent with your values. It should include value, inspiration, believability, and specificity while being easy to understand, relevant, and appropriate to the organization. It should serve a reason and guide your organization.

Good mission statements have similar characteristics. They are simple, captivating, measurable, relevant, and long-term. It's best to use common language that everyone understands and avoid using jargon or buzzwords.

A small business can create their Mission Statement by following these steps:

1. Understand the main components of a mission statement
    - State what your company does
    - List its top values
    - Offer the main goal accomplished when your company successfully fulfills its mission
2. Answer questions about your business
    - What products/services do you provide?
    - Who are your customers?
    - Where are your customers?
    - How do you make it possible?
    - What is the ultimate value/positive outcome of those products/services?
3. Gather ideas
    - Get input from employees, stakeholders, and customers to help shape your mission statement
4. Define your mission
    - Use the information gathered to define your company's mission in a clear and concise way
5. Create and finalize your draft
    - Write a draft of your mission statement and revise it until it accurately reflects your company's purpose

Jack set up this as his Mission Statement for his new company:

The New McKinley Family Logistics Company promises to exceed the services of any other trucking company by consistently delivering on our promise to provide timely and reliable supply of your required beverage shipments. We represent the market's best selection of products, thanks to our close relations with suppliers, and deliver them with care to ensure no breakage. We place a strong emphasis on building and maintaining great rapport with our customers, and providing exceptional service and support to meet and anticipate your needs. This dedication to customer satisfaction sets us apart from our competitors who experience untrained staff and high turnovers.

Set Your Marketing Goals

After completing his Mission Statement, Jack knew that setting marketing goals for his trucking and distribution company would help him attract more customers, drivers, and partners, as well as increase his new brand's awareness and reputation. He made sure that the goals were SMART: Specific, Measurable, Achievable, Relevant, and Time-bound. This gave Jack a way to plan his actions and strategies accordingly, and the ability to monitor his progress and results moving forward. He identified five opportunity areas for him to focus his marketing initiatives.

Jack wanted to increase his customer base

He felt the previous management had not attracted customers who had never used the trucking services. He decided to reach out to that market by offering competitive pricing, quality service, and customized solutions. He thought he also might leverage referrals, testimonials, and online reviews to showcase the company's credibility and reliability.

Jack prioritized attracting drivers

He knew that finding experienced, reliable drivers is often a challenge for trucking companies due to high job turnover. He decided he could use social media, job boards, and industry events to recruit qualified candidates.

Jack set the intention to increase marketing efforts

To reach more potential customers and partners, Jack knew he needed to increase his visibility and exposure in the market. He explored using various online and offline marketing channels, such as email marketing, videos, social media marketing, website optimization, SEO, content marketing, direct mail, flyers, brochures, and trade shows as possible outreach. He vowed to track and measure the effectiveness of the company's marketing campaigns and adjust them accordingly.

Jack also decided to improve online presence

He felt he needed to have a professional and user-friendly website that showcased their trucking and distribution services, values, and achievements. He wanted to see how he could optimize the website for search engines so that it ranked higher in relevant searches. He also laid plans to use social media platforms to engage with the company's potential audience, share useful information, and promote their brand.

Jack saw opportunity in expanding the service area

To grow his business and increase his revenue, Jack desired to expand the service area to new regions and look at new markets. First up, he researched the demand and competition in different areas and identified the best opportunities for the company. He also considered partnering with other trucking or distribution companies to offer more comprehensive solutions to his existing customers.

Craft Your Key Message

As a next step in his first of the *4 Points of Focus*, Jack knew he needed to craft a key message.

The NorthStar principle for key marketing messaging is that it is a concise and compelling statement that summarizes the value proposition of a company—in this case, Jack's trucking and distribution company.

The message needs to communicate:

- What you do
- How you do it
- Why you are different from your competitors

A key marketing message should also resonate with your target audience and persuade them to choose your company over others.

To craft his key marketing message, Jack needed to do some research and analysis on his company, their customers, and their competitors to ensure he understood his customer's needs, wants, and pain points, as well as their decision-making criteria. It was also important to identify his unique selling points, his distribution system's benefits and features, and the company's competitive advantages. He also needed to know how his competitors positioned themselves and what they offered. Based on his research and analysis, he could then write a key marketing message that highlighted the company's strengths, addressed the customer's problems, and differentiated the McKinley Family Logistics from their rivals.

The NorthStar method recommends a formula like this to structure your key marketing message:

[Your company name] is a [type of company] that [what you do]. Unlike [your competitors], we [how you do it differently]. This means [why it matters to your customers].

Make sure that your key marketing message is clear, concise, and consistent across all your marketing channels and materials.

Here is what Jack came up with for his company:

McKinley Family Logistics is a trucking and distribution company that provides reliable, efficient, and customized solutions for all your beverage transportation needs. Unlike other trucking companies, we have a large fleet of trucks and a spacious distribution center that can handle any size or type of cargo. This means you can save time, money, and hassle by choosing us as your one-stop partner for all your beverage and bottle trucking and distribution needs.

THE MARKETING BUDGET

It should be noted that none of the *4 Points of Focus* operate in a vacuum, and they often affect each other. In this case, an aspect of the Financial Point of Focus applies to the Marketing Point of Focus: The Marketing Budget.

An effective Marketing Budget is a plan that outlines how much money you will spend on your marketing activities and how you will allocate it across different channels, campaigns, and tools. This should be based on your marketing goals, expected revenue, and industry benchmarks. There is no definitive answer to what the "ideal" marketing budget for a small business should be; it depends on various factors such as the size of the company, stage of growth, industry trends, and competitive landscape.

Here, however, is a general guideline:

Established businesses should spend between 5% and 15% of their annual revenue on marketing, while new businesses may need to spend more to build their brand and customer base.

To craft a marketing budget for McKinley Family Logistics, Jack proceeded to follow these steps:

Jack estimated his revenue

Based on the company's past performance, market research, and growth projections, he estimated how much revenue he expected to generate in the next year. This told him how much he could afford to spend on marketing and what kind of return on investment (ROI) he needed to achieve.

Jack quantified his marketing goals

Jack took the five objectives of his marketing plan and applied their estimated costs and ROI into the budget.

Jack chose his marketing channels

Based on his target audience, his company's value proposition, and his competitive advantage, Jack chose the most effective and efficient marketing channels to reach and persuade his potential customers. To do this, he had to consider the costs and benefits of each channel and how they fit into his overall marketing strategy. Out of his previously outlined activities—email marketing, social media marketing, website optimization, SEO, content marketing, direct mail, flyers, brochures, and trade shows—he determined that heavy print costs for direct mail or brochures would not be effective, and prioritized other areas, particularly the beverage trade shows attended by his suppliers and customers.

Jack allocated his funds

Based on his revenue estimate, marketing goals, and chosen marketing channels, Jack allocated a specific amount of money to each channel and campaign. He also set aside some funds for contingency or unexpected expenses.

MEASURE YOUR RESULTS

Once you have implemented your budget, as Jack did in the previous example, you should monitor and measure the results of your marketing activities.

You should use Key Performance Indicators (KPIs) such as leads generated, conversions, sales, customer retention, and customer satisfaction to evaluate the effectiveness and efficiency of each channel or campaign. You should also compare the actual costs and revenues to the budgeted ones and identify any variances or gaps.

Based on the data and feedback you collect, you should adjust your budget as needed to optimize your ROI and achieve your goals.

Here are seven NorthStar tips for measuring and monitoring a marketing campaign.

1. <u>Start with a clear goal and objective</u>: You need to know what you want to achieve with your campaign, whether you wish to:
   - Raise brand awareness
   - Generate leads
   - Increase sales
   - Or something else

   As previously pointed out, your goal should be specific, measurable, achievable, realistic, and timely.

2. Decide what metrics to use: Your metrics should be aligned with your goal and the channels you use. For example,
   - If your goal is to increase brand awareness, you might use metrics like impressions, reach, traffic by source, or bounce rate.
   - If your goal is to generate leads, you might use metrics like conversions, cost per lead, and lead quality.
3. Establish a timeframe: Set a start and end date for your campaign and measure its performance over that period. You can also compare your results with previous campaigns or industry benchmarks.
4. Set a schedule to monitor campaign results: Develop and use an analytics tool to regularly track your metrics and see how they change over time.
5. Choose marketing tools to support your goals: Research and utilize the right tools for the right channels and tasks.
6. Use a marketing dashboard to present your results: Visualize your data and make it easy to understand and share. Different applications are available to help you create interactive dashboards that show your key metrics and insights.
7. Benchmark your performance data: Compare your results with your goals to see if you're meeting or exceeding them. You can also compare your results with industry standards or competitors' data to see how you're performing in the market.

WHAT IS A "TARGET MARKET" AND HOW DO YOU DEFINE YOURS?

We have mentioned the importance of defining your "target market." What exactly does that mean?

A target market is a specific group of potential customers that a business aims to reach with its products or services. This group may share common characteristics— age, gender, income level, education, interests, or geographic location—that make them more likely to be interested in, and purchase from, a business.

Here are the top five points to consider when defining your target market.

1. Demographics: Demographic segmentation is one of the classic segmentation tools.
2. Location: Where do the people in your target market live or do business?

3. <u>Socio-Cultural Profile:</u> Socio-cultural factors delve a little deeper into the demographics of your target, detailing aspects like lifestyle, attitudes, interests, and values.

4. <u>Digital Profile:</u> To a certain extent, the digital profile of your target will be linked to their age. A digital profile is a collection of information that exists online about an individual. It can describe a person's personality, behavior, interests, achievements, and interactions. It can also reflect a person's online brand, reputation, and career opportunities.

5. <u>Needs</u>: What new product will satisfy a need or solve a problem, or both, for this audience? Defining this aspect of your target market is crucial. You must determine their "hot button" needs, and align those with the solutions, services, or products you offer to meet those needs.

Jack's target market was determined by:

- Demographics of business owner profile (often a sports-oriented, middle-aged male)
- Location (within reach of his distribution centers)
- A beverage offering to consumers
- A need for a cost-effective and reliable supply chain with positive financing terms

BRANDING

Branding is the process of creating a unique image, name, and reputation for your business. It is critical to establish a brand identity that sets your business apart from the competition.

The importance of Branding in marketing cannot be overstated as it defines the overall experience your customers will associate with you. Simon Sinek states, "The goal is not just to sell to people who need what you have; the goal is to sell to people who believe what you believe." Your brand is what your customers, prospects, employees, and the public believe you are.

A well-executed brand strategy can increase your brand recognition, create an understanding of your value, and drive profitability.

Develop Your Unique Brand Identity

Developing a Unique Brand Identity requires a thorough understanding of your business, industry, target audience, and competitors. This process involves determining your company's values, mission, and vision, and establishing a brand personality that accurately reflects these principles.

Your brand identity should be consistent across all communication channels, from your website and social media profiles, to your product packaging and business cards, to how your personnel interact with prospects and customers. Creativity is vital during this process, but it must always be rooted in a clear understanding of your brand.

Your Brand Positioning Statement

Defining your Brand Positioning is a critical step in building a strong brand. Your Brand Positioning Statement should highlight the key elements of your brand identity. It should articulate the unique value that your business offers to your target audience and why they should choose your company over the others. It should be concise, memorable, and inform all aspects of your marketing strategy.

There are six methods that can help define your brand and create an identity that sets you apart from competitors.

1. Research: Understand your industry, market, and competition to create a unique brand message.
2. Assess your product or service benefits: What makes your offering different or better than other offerings? Highlighting unique selling points can help differentiate your brand.
3. Customer history: Understanding how your past customers interacted with your brand can help you tailor your messaging and positioning more effectively. If their perceptions differ greatly from your intentions, you can take direction in altering your messaging and/or re-assessing if your intended benefits meet reality.
4. Customer feedback: Beyond looking at patterns in customer history, ask them for direct feedback. This can provide you with valuable insights into how your brand is perceived and where there may be areas for improvement.
5. Surveys and focus groups: Bringing together a group of customers, or potential customers, in a focus group, or surveying a larger population of them, can give you a sense of what resonates with your target audience. This can help you fine-tune your messaging, packaging, and overall branding strategy.
6. Use online tools: The online world of social media can give you a virtual finger on the pulse of your brand. Google Alerts can monitor the web for mentions of your brand. Online reviews will give you further insights. Interaction with customers or prospects in social media posts is another great avenue.

Your brand should not stay static. Customer needs change, competitors may introduce innovations and disrupt your value, new technologies may be introduced that may work with you or against you. Staying creative and in touch with your customer needs will help you hone your brand—to keep it consistent and trusted, but at the same time, flexible and responsive.

Jack determined that the McKinley Family Logistics Company's customers needed a reliable fulfillment of the beverages they carried. They wanted replenishment as they needed it, not delivered early to be stored, or late and losing them consumer sales. They also wanted friendly sales representatives who were knowledgeable of the new beverages available, and provided guidance on how to sell them.

Jack set out to define his brand with a friendly and educated delivery force, tight and efficient delivery schedules, new inventory management systems tied into their customers inventories, and more. His brand said, "We will meet your needs and exceed your expectations."

DEFINING YOUR VALUE PROPOSITION

Your company's brand must reflect a deeper element of your product or service offering: its Value Proposition. Your Value Proposition is the statement that explains the benefits of your product or service to a customer or market segment.

The Proposition is an easy-to-understand reason why your prospective customer should buy the product or service from you. It serves as a declaration of intent, both inside your company and in the marketplace. It should clearly:

- Explain how a product fills a need
- Communicate the specifics of its added benefit
- State the reason why it's better than similar products or services in the market

The ideal Value Proposition is to-the-point and appeals to a customer's strongest decision-making drivers.

When a customer or prospect encounters your brand, your Value Proposition provides the impression you want them to walk away with. A strong Value Proposition should be embedded in your business mode and focus on areas your customers care about the most. It should differentiate you from the competition and be difficult for others to imitate. A strong Value Proposition can provide many benefits to your company:

- Make it easier for you to connect with target audience
- Establish a foundation for you to build your marketing and sales activities on
- Provide your employees with a consistent and cohesive way to talk about what they are doing

- Make your business distinct from the competition
- Attract and convert more customers
- Increase customer loyalty
- Command higher prices
- Outperform your competition
- Provide the foundation for your offering
- Create a strong differentiation between you and your competitors
- Increase the quantity and quality of prospective leads
- Help your organization internally by giving your staff a roadmap for success
- Clearly and concisely communicate what customers can gain from selecting your brand over that of your competitors

Your Value Proposition must be relevant to your company's values and your employees' needs to make them feel proud, motivated, and engaged.

To create a Value Proposition, follow these steps:

1. Identify all the benefits your product or service offers.
2. Describe what makes these benefits valuable.
3. Identify your customer's main problem.
4. Connect your value to your buyer's problem.
5. Differentiate yourself as the preferred provider of this value.

A Value Proposition should cover three elements:

- The promise of what you will deliver to your customers
- The benefits your customers will reap
- Why they should choose you over your competition

It should be among the first things website visitors see when they interact with your business, the first thing they hear when they are helped by your staff, and the first impression they get when meeting you.

Once you have a sense of what your value proposition entails, test it. Just as with your brand definition, which should reflect your value proposition, do not make assumptions. Here are some tips to test and validate your value proposition with real customers.

1. <u>Define your hypothesis</u>: Before you start testing your value proposition, you need to have a clear idea of what you want to learn and how you will measure it.

2. <u>Choose your testing method</u>: The methods you choose to test your value proposition with real customers can take many forms, depending on your goals, resources, and development stage. These can include focus groups, surveys, trend reports, and interviews by an unbiased third party, among other testing services.

3. <u>Segment your audience</u>: Make sure to test your value proposition with the right audience.

4. <u>Collect and analyze data</u>: Collect data from your tests and analyze it to see if your value proposition is resonating with your target audience.

5. <u>Iterate and improve</u>: Use the insights from your tests to improve your value proposition.

Jack determined that "flaky" beverage suppliers and uncaring service people were unresponsive to bar owners and store owners complaining about running out of popular beverages. When the orders were delivered, they often came all at once, leading to storage issues and the retailers needing to sell them at a reduced price to relieve inventory issues.

Jack was determined to make the McKinley Family Logistics Company the "relationship" company—to establish the best relations with suppliers, to get the right amount of product to retailers at the right time, and to offer them diversity of products and expand the breadth of what they could offer to their end consumers.

PRICING STRATEGY

A Pricing Strategy is a mission-critical plan, process, and methodology taken by businesses to decide how much to charge for their goods and services. The interaction between margin, price, and selling level is given specific consideration while pricing products.

There are several common pricing strategies to choose from to price products and services. These include competitive pricing strategy, dynamic pricing strategy, value-based pricing strategy, skimming pricing strategy, penetration pricing strategy, and economy pricing strategy. Here is a brief overview.

- <u>Competitive pricing strategy</u>: Prices products based on the price of competitive products, rather than cost or target profit—usually cheaper than competitors.

- <u>Dynamic pricing strategy</u>: Varies pricing based on marketing and customer demand.

- <u>Value-based pricing strategy</u>: Prices a product based on how much the customer believes it is worth.

- <u>Skimming pricing strategy</u>: Sets new product prices high and subsequently lowers them as competitors enter the market. It is the opposite of penetration pricing, which prices newly-launched products low to build a big customer base at the outset.

- <u>Penetration pricing strategy</u>: Enters a market at a low price and increases prices over time.

- <u>Economy pricing strategy</u>: Prices a product low because of low costs of production, marketing, and advertising, and relies on high sales volume to generate profit.

Pricing is a crucial aspect of a business' marketing strategy and is a significant element in the marketing mix. It can help to convey the value of a product or service to customers, attract customers, inspire customer trust and confidence, boost sales, increase revenue, and improve profit margins. On the other hand, a poorly thought-out pricing strategy can target the wrong customers, make them feel uncertain about trusting and buying your product, and inaccurately portray the value of your product.

Pricing influences the sales volume, profitability, and competitiveness of a product, potentially affecting the company's competitive position in the market. It reflects the corporate objectives and policies, and can be used to offset the weaknesses in other elements of the marketing mix. Opportunistic pricing strategies can help to increase sales and profits without having to spend more on marketing.

PROMOTIONAL MARKETING ASSETS AND THEIR IMPACT ON THE ENDGAME

Promotional methods deliver messages and offers to your target market; you will need to choose which ones are right for your business. Some of these methods bring greater value than simply distributing information as they can be utilized to establish an audience you own.

Email lists, website traffic, social media follower lists, Yelp/Google reviews, and YouTube channel subscribers can all be built as vehicles to deliver a company's marketing messaging. These various assets also become items of value and significance when the owner reaches the "endgame." The audience they represent and the pipeline to reach them can be valuable to a company, as well as valued by an entity wanting to purchase that company, simply because they would be expensive to build from scratch. Intangible qualities like credibility, trust, and familiarity also require huge investments to recreate.

WHAT EXPERTS SAY ABOUT MARKETING STRATEGIES AS A POINT OF FOCUS

Marketing is not just about selling products or services. It is about creating value, trust, and connection with your audience. It is about understanding their needs, desires, and motivations, and delivering solutions that make their lives better. Seth Godin, best-selling author and marketing guru, said, "What people want is the extra, the emotional bonus they get when they buy something they love."

To achieve this, business owners need to be creative, innovative, and authentic. They need to tell stories that resonate with their audience, not just share facts and features. Rather than only promote their brand, they need to use social media as a platform to engage, educate, and entertain their audience. They need to listen to their customers, not just talk at them. Jay Baer, an author and inspirational marketing speaker, said, "Content is fire. Social media is gasoline."

Bottom line, business owners need to lead the company in projecting the brand and value. Mostly, you need to care about your customers, your communities, and your impact on the world. You need to show empathy, compassion, and generosity, to create value that goes beyond the transaction. As entrepreneur, speaker, and marketing expert Gary Vaynerchuk said, "The best marketing strategy ever: CARE."

"Marketing is not a one-way street. It's a conversation. It's a relationship. It's a powerful way to make a difference."

–Pamela Vaughan

Get it right, and you will have succeeded on 25% of your *4 Points of Focus* journey.

SECTION 2: FINANCIAL STRUCTURE & GROWTH, THE GREEN POINT OF FOCUS

The second of the *4 Points of Focus* is Financial Structure & Growth. This Point of Focus is Green, symbolizing the growth and productivity this Point can bring you.

> *"The purpose of business is not to make money, it's to advance a greater purpose or cause."*
> –Simon Sinek

Financial systems are a means to an end—that end is the desire to create an environment where you and your business can thrive. When your financial system is working well, it will allow you and your business to take risks, expand, and create more jobs. This benefits your business, your employees, and your business' end value.

WHY FINANCIAL STRUCTURE & GROWTH ARE IMPORTANT FOR A HEALTHY BUSINESS

Financial Structure & Growth are the foundation of any healthy business. They provide the framework for managing a business' finances, from tracking income and expenses to making strategic financial decisions. A well-designed Financial Structure & Growth framework can help a business to:

- <u>Achieve its financial goals</u>: By tracking its financial performance, a business can identify areas where it is doing well. This information can then be used to make strategic decisions that will help the business achieve its financial goals.

- **Identify and manage risk**: Financial Structure & Growth helps a business to identify and manage risk. By understanding its financial exposure, a business can take steps to mitigate risk and protect its financial health. A well-designed financial structure can help to reduce risk by ensuring that the business has adequate financial resources to meet its obligations. This can protect the business from financial problems if unexpected events occur.

- **Make informed decisions**: By having access to accurate and timely financial information, a business can make informed decisions about its operations. This information can help the business to allocate resources efficiently, identify new opportunities, and respond to challenges.

- **Improved financial performance**: A well-managed financial system can help a business to track its financial performance and identify areas where it can improve. This can lead to increased profits and a stronger financial position.

There are several different financial systems that can be used to manage a business' finances. These systems can range from simple spreadsheets to complex Enterprise Resource Planning (ERP) systems. The right system will depend on the budget, size, and complexity of your business.

UNDERSTANDING THE DIFFERENT LEGAL FINANCIAL STRUCTURES FOR YOUR BUSINESS

You can form your business under a variety of legal structures. It is important to understand the benefits of each and determine which best meets your needs and objectives.

1. **Sole Proprietorship**: A Sole Proprietorship is the simplest type of business structure. It is owned and operated by one person, who is personally liable for all debts and obligations of the business. Sole Proprietorships are easy to set up and maintain, and they do not require any formal paperwork. However, the owner's personal assets are at risk if the business is sued or goes bankrupt.

   Benefits of a Sole Proprietorship:
   - Easy to set up and maintain
   - No formal paperwork required
   - Owner has complete control over the business
   - Owner is taxed on the business' profits as personal income

2. <u>General Partnership</u>: A General Partnership is a business owned by two or more people. The partners share the profits and losses of the business, and they are each personally liable for all debts and obligations of the business. General Partnerships are easy to set up, but they can be risky for the partners.

   Benefits of a General Partnership:
   - Easy to set up
   - No formal paperwork required
   - Partners share the profits and losses of the business
   - A partnership agreement is required

   Another form of a partnership is an LLP or Limited Liability Partnership. It has the same characteristic of a general partnership, but the partners do have limited personal liability for the debts of the partnership.

3. <u>Limited Liability Company (LLC)</u>: An LLC is a hybrid business structure that offers the limited liability of a corporation and the flexibility of a partnership. The owners of an LLC are called "members," and are not personally liable for the debts and obligations of the business. LLCs are more complex to set up than sole proprietorships or partnerships, but they offer more protection for the owners.

   Benefits of an LLC:
   - Limited liability for the owners
   - Flexibility of a partnership
   - Easy to transfer ownership
   - Can be taxed as a corporation or a partnership
   - An operating agreement is required

4. <u>Corporation</u>: A Corporation is a legal entity that is separate from its owners. The owners of a corporation are called shareholders, and are not personally liable for the debts and obligations of the corporation. Corporations are more complex to set up and maintain than other business structures, but they offer the most protection for the owners.

   Benefits of a Corporation:
   - Limited liability for the owners
   - Ability to raise capital through the sale of stock
   - Long-term existence
   - Ease of transferring ownership

a. <u>S Corporation:</u> An S Corporation is a type of corporation that elects to be taxed as a pass-through entity. This means that the profits and losses of the corporation are passed through to the shareholders, who are taxed on their personal income tax returns. S Corporations offer the limited liability of a corporation with the tax benefits of a partnership.

Benefits of an S Corporation:

- Limited liability for the owners
- Taxed as a pass-through entity
- Easy to set up and maintain
- Can be owned by a limited number of shareholders

b. <u>C Corporation</u>: A C Corporation is a type of corporation that is taxed as a separate entity from its owners. The profits and losses of the corporation are taxed on the corporation's income tax return. C Corporations offer the most flexibility for raising capital and expanding the business, but they can also have one of the higher tax liabilities.

Benefits of a C Corporation:

- Flexibility for raising capital
- Ability to expand the business
- Highest degree of ownership control

5. <u>Cooperative</u>: A Cooperative is a business owned and operated by its members. The members share the profits and losses of the business, and they are each personally liable for a share of the business' debts. Cooperatives are often formed by groups of people who share a common interest, such as farmers or consumers.

Benefits of a Cooperative:

- Members share in the profits and losses of the business
- Members have control over the business
- Can be used to provide goods or services to members

6. <u>Nonprofit Corporation</u>: A Nonprofit Corporation is a business that is organized for charitable or educational purposes. Nonprofit Corporations are not taxed on their profits, and they are not allowed to distribute profits to their members. Nonprofit Corporations are often formed to provide social services, such as running a soup kitchen or providing legal aid.

Benefits of a Nonprofit Corporation:

- Not taxed on profits
- Not allowed to distribute profits to members
- Can provide social services

The best business structure for you will depend on your individual circumstances and goals. If you are starting a small business with limited liability concerns, a Sole Proprietorship or LLC may be a good option. If you are looking to raise capital or expand your business, a Corporation may be a better choice. If you are interested in forming a Cooperative or Nonprofit Corporation, you will need to do some additional research to determine if these structures are right for you.

Jack of McKinley Family Logistics elected to form an LLC. He set his goals to build the company to the point that it was a thriving and robust business so he could then sell it and transfer its ownership through the acquisition. The LLC structure would enable him to do so when the time came.

WHY YOU NEED A SOLID FINANCIAL SYSTEM AS THE FOUNDATION OF YOUR BUSINESS

A solid Financial System is essential for any business, regardless of size or industry. It provides the foundation for making informed decisions, managing cash flow, and ensuring long-term financial health. The abilities of a healthy system include:

- <u>Tracking income and expenses</u>: A good Financial System will track all your income and expenses, so you can see where your money is going and ensure you're not overspending in any areas.

- <u>Creating budgets and forecasts</u>: A Financial System can help you create budgets and forecasts, which will give you a better understanding of your financial future. This will help you make better decisions about how to allocate your resources.

- <u>Managing cash flow</u>: Cash flow is the lifeblood of any business, and a good Financial System will help you manage it effectively. This assists you to avoid running out of cash, and ensures that you have enough money to pay your bills on time.

- <u>Complying with regulations</u>: Many businesses are required to comply with financial and tax regulations. A good Financial System will help you track your financial activity and ensure that you're in compliance.

- Making better decisions: A good Financial System will provide you with the information you need to make better decisions about your business. This could include decisions about pricing, marketing, or expansion.

Clearly, a good Financial System is important to your company. Specific and important benefits that demonstrate why your Financial System is a key NorthStar Point of Focus, include:

- Increased profitability: A good Financial System can help you identify areas where you can save money or increase revenue. This can lead to increased profitability for your business.

- Improved cash flow management: A good Financial System will help you manage your cash flow effectively. This will help you avoid running out of cash and ensure that you have enough money to pay your bills on time.

- Reduced risk: A good Financial System can help you reduce your risk by providing you with the information you need to make informed decisions. This could include decisions about pricing, marketing, or expansion.

- Improved decision-making: A good Financial System will provide you with the information you need to make better decisions about your business.

While having a healthy Financial System propels you towards your North Star and ultimate success, NOT having a good system can lead to some serious ramifications. The downfalls of not having a good Financial System include:

- Financial problems: If you don't have a good Financial System, you're more likely to experience financial problems. This could include running out of cash, not being able to pay your bills on time, or even going bankrupt.

- Poor decision-making: If you don't have a good Financial System, you're more likely to make poor decisions about your business. This could lead to missed opportunities, increased costs, or even the failure of your business.

- Compliance issues: If you don't have a good Financial System, you're more likely to have compliance issues. This could lead to fines, penalties, or even the loss of your business license.

There is a tragic history of big companies being brought down by Financial Systems that failed.

Enron was a large energy company that collapsed in 2001. The company had a complex financial system that was not properly audited, which allowed the company to hide billions of dollars in debt and artificially inflate its profits.

WorldCom was a telecommunications company that collapsed in 2002. Like Enron, WorldCom also had a complex financial system that was not properly audited, which allowed the company to overstate its revenues and hide billions of dollars in expenses.

Lehman Brothers was a large investment bank that collapsed in 2008 during the Financial Crisis. This company had a complex financial system that was not properly managed, which allowed the company to take on too much risk and eventually go bankrupt.

The cautionary tale here is that even the giants, the companies perceived as the "biggest and the best," can be brought down to rubble without a strong and respected financial system. Don't be an Enron, WorldCom, or Lehman.

HOW TO USE YOUR FINANCIAL STATEMENTS TO TELL THE STORY OF YOUR BUSINESS

A Financial Statement is a report that shows your financial activities and business performance. Among other uses, lenders and investors can utilize it to check your business' earning potential as well as its overall health.

There are three main types of financial statements:

- <u>Income statement:</u> This statement shows a company's revenues and expenses over a period of time, such as a year or a quarter. It tells you whether a company is making a profit or a loss.

- <u>Balance sheet:</u> This statement shows a company's assets, liabilities, and shareholders' equity at a specific point in time. It tells you what a company owns, what it owes, and what its net worth is.

- <u>Cash flow statement:</u> This statement shows how much cash a company generates and uses over a period of time. It tells you how well a company is managing its cash flow.

Your Financial Statements can tell the story of your business. Your income statement might show that your revenue has been growing steadily over the past few years. This could be a sign that the company is doing well and that your products or services are in demand. Your balance sheet might show that your assets have increased significantly over the past few years. This could be a sign that the company is investing in the future and that it is a growing business. Your cash flow statement might show that your cash flow has been positive for the past few years. This could be a sign that the company is managing its finances well and that you have enough cash to meet your obligations.

By carefully reading a company's Financial Statements, you can learn a lot about its financial health and performance. This information can be valuable for investors, lenders, and other stakeholders who are interested in the company.

Of course, Financial Structure & Growth statements reflect just one of the *4 Points of Focus* and are a foundational piece of the puzzle when it comes to understanding a company. They can point to the need to test your tone from the top as leader, your company's management team, your agility around the competitive landscape, and your reactions to industry trends. Financial Statements can provide a valuable starting point for understanding your financial health and performance.

Five great NorthStar tips for gaining insight and value when reading your Financial Statements:

- Be sure to understand the different types of Financial Statements and what they mean.
- Compare the company's financial statements over time to see how it is performing.
- Compare the company's financial statements to those of its competitors.
- Look for trends in the company's financial statements.
- Consult with a financial advisor if you need help understanding financial statements.

WHAT AN INCOME STATEMENT IS AND WHAT IT TELLS YOU

An Income Statement is a financial statement that summarizes your company's revenues, expenses, and profits over a period of time. It is also sometimes called a profit-and-loss statement (P&L), or an earnings statement. The Income Statement typically has the following features:

- Revenue: This is the amount of money that your company generates from its sales of goods or services.
- Cost of goods sold (COGS): This is the direct cost of producing the goods or services that your company sells.

- Gross profit: This is the difference between revenue and COGS.

- Operating expenses: These are the expenses that your company incurs, such as rent, salaries, and marketing costs, in order to operate its business.

- Net income: This is your company's profit after all expenses have been deducted.

Familiarity with your Income Statement, and using it as a valued tool, gives you a snapshot of your company's financial performance which can benefit you in a number of ways. The Income Statement shows how much money your company is making or losing, and it can help to identify areas where the company can improve its profitability. It is used by investors and lenders to assess the company's financial health. It can also help your management team to make decisions about your company's operations. They can identify areas where the company is spending too much money and track the company's progress towards its financial goals.

HOW YOUR BALANCE SHEET HELPS YOU UNDERSTAND YOUR ASSETS, LIABILITIES, AND EQUITY

A Balance Sheet is a financial statement that provides a snapshot of your company's assets, liabilities, and equity at a specific point in time. It does not reflect changes in the company's financial position over time. The Balance Sheet is prepared using the accrual basis of accounting which means that assets and liabilities are recorded when they are earned or incurred, not when they are received or paid.

The assets are listed on the left side of the Balance Sheet, the liabilities are listed on the right side, and the equity is the difference between the two as noted in the formula $A - L = E$ or $A = L + E$. Both formulas are looking at the same information, just from a slightly different perspective.

Assets (A): Assets are resources that your company owns and that have economic value. They can be classified as either current assets or long-term assets. Current assets are assets that are expected to be converted into cash within one year, such as cash, accounts receivable, and inventory. Long-term assets are assets that have a useful life of more than one year, such as land, buildings, and equipment.

Liabilities (L): Liabilities are debts that your company owes to others. They too can be classified as either current or long-term. Current liabilities are debts that are due within one year, such as accounts payable, accrued expenses, and short-term debt. Long-term liabilities are debts that are due more than one year from the current time period, such as bonds payable and long-term debt.

Equity (E): Equity is the ownership interest in your company and is the difference between your company's assets and liabilities. Equity can be divided into two categories: contributed capital and retained earnings. Contributed capital is the money that investors have invested in the company. Retained earnings are the profits that the company has earned over time and that have not been paid out to shareholders in the form of dividends or distributions.

The Balance Sheet is a vital and valuable tool for understanding your company's financial position. It provides information about your company's assets, liabilities, and equity, which can be used to assess your company's liquidity, solvency, and financial strength.

Liquidity: Liquidity is the ability of your company to meet its short-term obligations. If your company has a high level of liquidity, it will be able to pay its bills on time and be less likely to experience financial difficulty.

Solvency: Solvency is the ability of your company to meet its long-term obligations. If your company has a high level of solvency, you will be able to pay its debts over time and be less likely to go bankrupt.

Financial Strength: Financial strength is the overall health of your company's financial position. If your company holds strong financial strength, it will be able to withstand financial shocks in economic downturns.

By carefully watching your balance sheet, you can make better financial decisions and improve your financial performance.

USING YOUR CASH FLOW STATEMENT IN A CASH MANAGEMENT BEST PRACTICE

Your Cash Flow Statement is a financial statement that summarizes the cash inflows and outflows of your company over a period of time. It is one of the three main financial statements we have discussed, along with the income statement and the balance sheet. The Cash Flow Statement provides information about how your company is generating and using cash, which can be used to assess your financial health and make decisions about your future.

A Cash Flow Statement is divided into three sections:

- <u>Operating activities</u>: Shows the cash flows generated by your company's core business activities, such as selling goods or services, collecting payments from customers, and paying suppliers.

- Investing activities: Shows the cash flows generated by your company's investment activities, such as buying or selling assets, and making or receiving investments.

- Financing activities: Shows the cash flows generated by your company's financing activities, such as issuing debt, repaying debt, issuing, or buying back shares, and paying dividends.

There are a number of cash management best practices that companies can deploy by using their Cash Flow Statement. The Cash Flow Statement can help you identify your main sources of cash, such as sales revenue, customer payments, and investments. With this information, you can develop strategies to increase cash flow from these sources.

The Cash Flow Statement can also help you identify your main cash outflows, such as expenses, debt payments, and dividends. With this information, you can figure out how to reduce cash outflows or to delay them until a later date.

You can also use the Cash Flow Statement to forecast future cash needs. This information can be used to ensure that you have enough cash on hand to meet your obligations.

It is also important that you use the Cash Flow Statement to monitor trends in cash flow. This enables you to identify potential problems early on and to take corrective action. Analyze your Cash Flow Statement over time. This will help you to identify trends and make informed decisions about your company's future. Use the Cash Flow Statement to set financial goals.

NorthStar Strategic Partners recommends working with three cash flow statements and plans: a year plan, a quarterly plan, and a monthly plan. In each, we will talk about the gross profit margin, the net profit margin, and your working capital ratio.

You will find the most pertinent information when you use all the financial tools together. Compare the cash flow statement to the income statement and balance sheet. You will be able to identify any discrepancies between the three statements, and fully understand what is impacting the company's cash and financial position and how it affects the business.

PROFIT

Being profitable is an obvious goal for a successful business, but what exactly does "profit" mean, and at what level are you being "successful?" Your company may be earning income, but what of that income is "profit?" There are two kinds of profit to consider: Gross Profit and Net Profit.

Gross Profit: Gross Profit is the profit your company makes after subtracting the Cost Of Goods Sold (COGS) from your revenue. COGS is the direct cost of producing the goods or services that your company sells. For example, if your company sells widgets, COGS will include the cost of the materials used to make the widgets, as well as the labor costs involved in making them.

Net Profit: Net Profit is the profit your company makes after subtracting all your expenses from your revenue. Expenses include COGS, as well as other costs such as marketing, sales, and administration. Net Profit is also known as net income or "the bottom line."

Therefore, the difference between gross and net profit is that Gross Profit only considers the costs directly related to producing the goods or services. Net Profit, on the other hand, considers all of a company's expenses, including both direct and indirect costs.

Here is an example of how to calculate Gross Profit and Net Profit:

Revenue	$1000
COGS	$250
Gross Profit	$750
Operating Expenses	$500
Net Profit	$250

- In this example, the company has a Gross Profit of $750 because it made $1000 in revenue and had $250 in COGS.

- The company's Net Profit is $250 because it had $750 in Gross Profit and $500 in operating expenses.

Gross Profit and Net Profit are both important metrics for measuring your company's profitability. Gross Profit tells you how much money your company makes from its core business activities, while Net Profit tells you how much money your company makes after all its expenses have been paid.

In the above example, if the company looked only at their Gross Profit, they might feel they were highly profitable. Their operating expenses are fairly high, however, so the Net Profit calculation tells them a different story.

Investors and analysts use Gross Profit and Net Profit to assess a company's financial health and to compare its performance to other companies in the same industry. Gross Profit and Net Profit are also used to calculate other financial metrics, such as Return On Equity (ROE) and Return On Assets (ROA).

A high Gross Profit margin indicates that your company is efficient in its production and/or distribution costs and indicates that you are efficient in overall operations and can control your expenses. What is considered a "high" profit margin will vary depending on the industry and your company's specific business model. As a general rule, a Net Profit margin of 20% or more is considered healthy (depending on your industry), and should be your target.

There are a number of ways to achieve a healthy profit margin. Probably the most obvious is to do the following three things in tandem:

- Increase sales: Expand into new markets, develop new products or services, or increase prices.
- Reduce costs: Negotiate better deals with suppliers, streamline operations, or reduce unnecessary expenses.
- Improve efficiency: Invest in new technology, train employees, or streamline processes.

Return On Assets

Besides the formula to measure profit margin, you can also calculate your Return On Assets (ROA). ROA is a measure of how much profit you generate from your assets. To calculate it, divide your company's profit by its total assets. If your company has shareholders, you also may want to calculate your Return On Equity (ROE). To figure this out, you need to know your company's net income and shareholders' equity. Once you have these two numbers, you can divide net income by shareholders' equity to calculate your ROE.

Once you have set a goal for your profit margin, you will need to measure your success on a regular basis.

KEY TIPS FOR YOUR BUSINESS TO MANAGE GROWTH AND MAINTAIN STABILITY THROUGH YOUR FINANCIAL STRUCTURE & GROWTH POINT OF FOCUS

Here are some tips for your business to manage growth and maintain stability with financial planning:

- Create a financial plan: This should include your goals for the business, as well as a projection of your income and expenses. It's important to regularly review and update your financial plan as your business grows and changes.

- Track your cash flow: This will help you stay on top of your incoming and outgoing money and identify any potential problems. There are a number of different tools and software programs that can help you track your cash flow.

- Minimize your overhead costs: This will help you keep your profits high and your business stable. Look for ways to reduce your rent, utilities, and other fixed costs.

- Invest in growth: If you want your business to grow, you need to be willing to invest in it. This could mean hiring new employees, expanding your product line, or opening a new location.

- Be prepared for unexpected expenses: Things happen, and sometimes businesses must deal with unexpected expenses. Make sure you have a contingency fund set aside so that you can cover these expenses without putting your business in jeopardy.

- Get professional assistance: If you're not comfortable managing your own finances, don't be afraid to get help from a professional accountant, financial advisor, or hire NorthStar Strategic Partners or other qualified firms. We can help you create a financial plan, track your cash flow, and make sure your business is on track.

- Pay yourself a salary: This may seem counterintuitive, but paying yourself a salary will help you track your business's profitability and ensure that you're taking home a fair share of the profits.

- Don't be afraid to borrow money: If you need to borrow money to grow your business, don't be afraid to do so. Just make sure you do your research and get the best terms possible. NorthStar Strategic Partners can help you evaluate options.

- Build good credit: Good credit will help you get loans, lines of credit, and other financing when you need it.

- Stay organized: Keep your financial records organized and up to date. This will make it easier to track your finances and make informed decisions about your business.

As mentioned, our friend Jack of the McKinley Family Logistics Company created an LLC as the financial structure of the company. The distribution company was originally a sole proprietorship, which meant that the owners were personally liable for any debts or legal issues that the company incurred. This was a risky proposition, as it could have put Jack's personal assets at risk.

By creating an LLC, Jack limited his personal liability to the assets of the company. This gave him peace of mind and made it easier for him to attract investors and lenders.

Jack also created a productive financial plan for his company. This plan included goals for revenue growth, profit margins, and cash flow. Jack tracked his progress against these goals on a regular basis and made adjustments as needed. The financial plan helped Jack to make better decisions about how to allocate the company's resources between the different distribution centers. It also helped him to identify potential risks and opportunities.

The combination of creating an LLC and following a productive financial plan helped Jack to grow his distribution company significantly. The company's revenue increased by 20% each year for the past three years. Profit margins also increased by 10% each year.

Jack was able to attract new investors and lenders, which gave him the capital to expand the company's fleet of trucks. He also opened some new distribution centers in several key markets.

Managing the finances of your business can be challenging, but it's essential for long-term success. By giving this Green Point of Focus thorough attention, you can help your business grow and thrive. A good financial structure will give you the vision to work within a sound budget that tracks your spending and the means to pay down debt while saving for the future. With an efficient and effective financial structure, you can invest in your business.

WHAT EXPERTS SAY ABOUT THE FINANCIAL STRUCTURE & GROWTH POINT OF FOCUS

Here are words of wisdom from financial experts:

"The worst sort of business is one that grows rapidly, requires significant capital to engender the growth and then earns little or no money."
—Warren Buffett, Chairman and CEO of
Berkshire Hathaway, 2007 Shareholder Letter

"Don't do anything stupid, and don't waste money. Let everybody else waste money and do stupid things, then we'll buy them."
—Jamie Dimon, Chairman and CEO of JPMorgan Chase

"Look for small companies that are already profitable and have proven that their concept can be replicated. Be suspicious of companies with growth rates of 50 to 100 percent a year."

—Peter Lynch, Former Investment Manager of Fidelity Magellan Fund

SECTION 3: OPERATIONAL EXCELLENCE, THE ORANGE POINT OF FOCUS

"Bad leaders care about who's right. Good leaders care about what's right."
–Simon Sinek

The third of the *4 Points of Focus* is Operational Excellence, where the compass directs your attention to your:

- Operations
- Processes and Systems
- Quality
- Desire to strive for continuous improvement

Its color is Orange, representing vibrancy and innovation.

Innovation is the lifeblood of any successful business, but it is especially important for small businesses. To stay ahead of the curve in today's competitive marketplace, small businesses need to be constantly innovating. When mentioning innovation, many business owners immediately go to ideas on how to develop new products or services, or new ways to market and sell. But innovation is not just about creating new products or services. Certainly, these are great ways to keep your business vibrant, but equally, and sometimes more importantly, are innovations in your operations, such as finding new ways to streamline your processes or improve your customer service. Innovation is about finding new ways to do things better.

There are many benefits in seeking to innovate your small business operations. Innovation can help you to increase your sales and profits, improve your competitive position, and keep existing customers happy—which then attracts new customers through referrals, improves your efficiency, and allows you to become more sustainable.

Innovation is not without its challenges. It can be risky and difficult to implement new ideas. However, the potential rewards of innovation are great. Small businesses willing to innovate are more likely to succeed in the long run.

Here are some additional thoughts to consider about the value of innovation in your small business operations:

- Innovation is not just for big businesses: small businesses can be just as innovative as big businesses, if not more so.
- Innovation is not about being perfect: it is about being willing to try new things and learn from your mistakes.
- Innovation is not a one-time event: it is an ongoing process that requires constant creativity and problem-solving.

Innovation is a mindset that the *4 Points of Focus* recommend in your pursuit of Operational Excellence. In order to apply it, however, we need to understand exactly what "Operational Excellence" is, and how it applies across an organization.

Operational Excellence is a business approach that emphasizes continuous improvement across all aspects of the business and within all business processes. The goal of Operational Excellence is to achieve the highest possible level of performance and efficiency, while minimizing waste and errors.

Operational Excellence is a relatively new concept in business, but it has its roots in earlier management philosophies such as Scientific Management, Total Quality Management (TQM), and Lean Manufacturing. These philosophies all focused on the importance of continuous improvement and waste reduction, and they laid the foundation for the development of the "Operational Excellence" we know today.

The term "Operational Excellence" was first coined in the early 1990s, and quickly gained popularity among businesses looking for ways to improve their performance. In the years since, Operational Excellence has become an essential component of many successful businesses.

Operational Excellence applies in four key areas within your business:

- <u>Strategy Development</u>: The first step to Operational Excellence is to develop a clear and concise strategy that outlines your organization's goals and objectives. This strategy should be based on a deep understanding of your organization's customers and their needs.
- <u>Process Excellence</u>: The next area of Operational Excellence is process excellence. This involves identifying and improving the key

processes that drive the organization's performance and making sure that systems speak to each other, elevating their data and creating knowledge.

- <u>Performance Management</u>: Once the strategy is in place and processes are defined, it is important to develop a system for measuring and monitoring performance. This will help to identify areas where improvement is needed, and to track progress over time.

- <u>Leadership and Culture</u>: Operational Excellence requires a strong commitment from leadership and a culture that supports continuous improvement. Leaders must create an environment where employees are empowered to make suggestions and to take ownership of their work.

Operational Excellence is a complex and challenging undertaking, but it can be highly rewarding. By implementing the principles of Operational Excellence, your business can achieve significant improvements in performance, efficiency, and profitability.

Improvements you can expect in your business thanks to achievement of Operational Excellence include:

- Increased customer satisfaction
- Reduced costs
- Improved efficiency
- Increased productivity
- Enhanced employee morale
- Improved decision-making
- Increased competitiveness

BEING STRATEGIC

Beginning your journey to Operational Excellence requires a strategy, a plan. To know where you are going, you first must assess where you are.

Use a variety of data sources to gather feedback. This could include customer surveys, employee surveys, financial reports, and industry benchmarking data. Involve employees in the process of identifying areas of improvement and developing solutions; this will help to ensure that changes are implemented effectively and that your employees are committed to the process.

Be willing to experiment with new ideas. There is no one-size-fits-all approach to Operational Excellence. The best approach for your business will depend on your specific needs and goals. Don't be afraid to make mistakes because everyone does this along the way; the important thing is to learn from your mistakes and keep moving forward.

Here is a recommended process to outline your Operational Point of Focus plan:

1. Identify areas where you want accomplishment: The first step is to identify the areas in which you want to experience greater accomplishments. This can be done by looking at your financial performance, customer feedback, and employee satisfaction surveys. You can also use benchmarking to compare your performance to other businesses in your industry.

2. Research key factors: There are a number of key factors that businesses need to research when identifying areas of improvement, creating a strategy for Operational Excellence, and developing and implementing processes. These factors include:
    - Customer needs and expectations
    - Industry best practices
    - Technological advances
    - Regulatory requirements

3. Set clear goals: Your goals for growth should be clear, measurable, achievable, relevant, and time bound. This will help you track your progress and ensure that you are on track to achieve your desired results.

4. Use data to drive accomplishment: Data can be a valuable tool for identifying areas where you can reach accomplishment, and measure effectiveness. Your accounting system should be a truth teller of your company's story and can be used to identify areas of your operation that are ineffective, cost too much, and drain profits. You can use data to track customer satisfaction, employee productivity, and financial performance.

5. Create a strategy for Operational Excellence: Once you have identified the areas that need improvement, you need to create a strategy for Operational Excellence. This strategy should outline your goals for improvement, the steps you will take to achieve those goals, and the resources you will need.

6. Develop and implement processes: The next step is to develop and implement processes that will help you achieve your goals. These processes should be clear, concise, and easy to follow. They should also be regularly reviewed and updated to ensure that they are still effective.

7. Gather feedback: It is important to gather feedback from a variety of sources, including customers, employees, and suppliers. This feedback can help you identify areas of improvement and ensure that your processes are meeting the needs of all stakeholders.

8. Communicate with stakeholders: It is important to communicate your plans for improvement with all stakeholders. This will help to ensure that everyone is on the same page and that there is buy-in for the changes.

9. Be patient and persistent: It takes time and effort to achieve operational excellence. Don't get discouraged if you don't see results immediately. Just keep working at it and you will eventually reach your goals.

10. Celebrate your successes: It is important to celebrate your successes along the way. This will help to keep you motivated and focused on your goals.

SET YOUR KEY PERFORMANCE INDICATORS (KPIs)

Key Performance Indicators (KPIs) are measurable values that indicate how well your business is performing against its goals. They can be used to track progress, identify areas for improvement, and make strategic decisions.

There are many different KPIs that can be used by small businesses, but some of the most common include:

- Revenue: the total amount of money that a business brings in during a given period of time.

- Profit: the amount of money that a business makes after all its expenses have been paid.

- Customer acquisition cost: the cost of acquiring a new customer.

- Customer lifetime value: the total amount of money that a customer is expected to spend with a business over the course of their relationship.

- Churn rate: the percentage of customers that stop doing business with a company within a given period of time.

- Employee satisfaction: a measure of how happy employees are with their jobs.

- Productivity: a measure of how much work is being done by employees in a given amount of time.

- <u>Market share</u>: the percentage of the market that a business controls.

Start with a few key KPIs, but don't try to track too many at once. Start with the ones that are most important to your business and that you can easily track. Your KPIs should be specific, measurable, achievable, relevant, and time-bound. You need to track your KPIs regularly in order to see how you are doing and make adjustments as needed. Your KPIs should be used to make strategic decisions about your business.

KPIs can be a valuable tool for small businesses of all sizes. By tracking the right KPIs and using them to make decisions, businesses can improve their performance and achieve their goals.

CREATING OPERATIONAL PROCESSES AND SYSTEMS FOR OPTIMAL PERFORMANCE AND EFFICIENCY

Once your strategies are defined and you have your KPIs in place, your plan will help you define and create excellence through well-defined operational processes and systems. These processes and systems should streamline workflows, eliminate redundancies, and improve communication. By doing so, your business can free up time and resources that can be used to focus on growth and innovation.

There are a number of steps involved in creating effective operational processes and systems. It is important to identify the key processes that need to be improved. Once these processes have been identified, it is necessary to map out the current process and identify areas where it is falling short. Next, set clear goals for the improvement process. Then implement the changes and monitor the results to ensure that the desired improvements have been achieved.

Involve all stakeholders in your operational mission. This will help to ensure that the new processes are well understood and supported by everyone involved. Use simple, easy-to-understand language. As you develop new processes, make sure they are clear and concise so that everyone can easily follow them

Get feedback from employees. Once the new processes are in place, ask employees for feedback on how they are working. This feedback can be used to make further improvements.

Be prepared to make changes. As the business grows and changes, the operational processes and systems will need to be updated as well.

Here are the key areas within your business that have systems and processes for you to identify, map, look for areas of improvement, change, then measure and monitor:

- **Customer Service**: This is one of the most important systems for any business as it directly affects customer satisfaction. Make sure your customer service processes are efficient and effective, and that your employees are empowered to resolve customer issues quickly and smoothly.

- **Order Fulfillment**: This system encompasses all the steps involved in getting a product or service to the customer, from order processing to shipping and delivery. Make sure your order fulfillment processes are streamlined and efficient, and that you have a clear understanding of your customers' expectations.

- **Inventory Management**: This system tracks the flow of inventory in and out of your business. A well-managed inventory system can help you reduce costs, improve customer service, and avoid stockouts.

- **Production/Manufacturing**: If your business produces or manufactures products, you need to have a well-designed production or manufacturing system in place. This system should ensure that your products are produced efficiently and to a high standard.

- **Job Costing**: Construction companies and others need to make sure their project-based operations are accurate and reflect projections that do not put the company at risk of losing money or being unable to effectively complete a project.

- **Procurement**: This system is responsible for acquiring the goods and services your business needs to operate. Make sure your procurement processes are efficient and effective, and that you are getting the best possible prices from your suppliers.

- **Information Technology**: This system encompasses all the technology that your business uses, from computers and software to networks and telecommunications. Make sure your IT systems are reliable and secure, and that they are aligned with your business needs.

For service businesses, Operational Excellence encompasses even more complexity. A strong element of this Point of Focus will be the customer experience, as this is everything in a service-based business. Your processes must be designed to deliver a positive and memorable customer experience. Within this environment, you must be flexible and adaptable. Things change quickly in the service industry so be prepared to adapt your processes to meet the changing needs of your customers.

If you are a service business, here are other areas that have systems and processes for you to identify, map, look for areas of improvement, change, then measure and monitor:

- Service Delivery: This system encompasses all the steps involved in delivering a service to the customer, from initial contact to follow-up. Make sure your service delivery processes are efficient and effective, and that your employees can deliver a high-quality service.

- Knowledge Management: This system is responsible for capturing and sharing knowledge within your organization. This can help you improve your service delivery, reduce errors, and resolve customer issues more quickly.

- Process Improvement: This system is responsible for identifying and implementing improvements to your service delivery processes, which can help you make your services more efficient, effective, and customer centric.

- Customer Feedback: This system is responsible for gathering and analyzing customer feedback, which can help you identify areas for improvement and improve your services.

In each of your functional areas, as outlined above, take these next three steps:

- Identify your business activities within the functional area
  Identify all the activities that your business needs to perform in order to operate the function.

- Break down each activity into steps
  Once you have identified your business activities, you need to break them down into smaller steps. This will help you to understand the flow of work and identify any potential bottlenecks.

- Document your systems and processes
  Once you have broken down your business activities into steps, you need to document your systems and processes. This will help you to communicate your processes to your team and ensure that everyone is on the same page.

Be highly mindful that none of the systems and processes in your business should operate in a vacuum. For true Operational Excellence to be achieved, they need to connect and elevate the data each collects. For example, if operating as it should, your accounting system can be the true storyteller of the health of your whole organization. That data needs to be integrated into relevant systems so it can have both immediate reactive, and proactive, effects.

System Integration

The different parts of your business should be able to communicate with each other seamlessly, so you get the most out of your data and make informed decisions about your business.

Another example: if you have a Customer Relationship Management (CRM) system, you will integrate it with your sales and marketing systems so you can track customer interactions across all channels. This will give you a complete view of your customers and allow you to provide them with a more personalized experience.

Here are three key reasons you need to connect and integrate your systems and processes:

- Increased Efficiency: When your systems are integrated, you can automate tasks and streamline your workflows. This can save you time and money, while also helping you improve your customer service.
- Improved Decision-making: When you have access to all your data in one place, you can make better decisions about your business because you will have a better understanding of your customers, your competitors, and your market.
- Enhanced Security: When your systems are integrated, it is easier to protect your data. This is because you can implement security measures across all your systems, rather than having to do it separately for each system.

The steps needed for System Integration will vary depending on the specific systems that you are integrating. Start small; don't try to integrate all your systems at once. Start with a few key systems, then build on your success. It is recommended that you get help from a professional like NorthStar Strategic Partners. If you're not sure how to integrate your systems, we can help you. System Integration can be a complex process so be patient and don't expect everything to happen overnight.

Here are some general steps to follow:

1. Assess your current systems and processes: This will help you identify which systems need to be integrated and how they should be integrated.

2. Choose the right integration solution: There are a number of different integration solutions available, so you will need to choose one that is right for your business.

3. Implement the integration solution: This will involve configuring the integration solution and testing it to make sure that it is working properly.

4. Train your staff on the new system: Your staff will need to be trained on how to use the new system so they can continue to work efficiently.

MANAGING YOUR OPERATIONAL PERFORMANCE

Once you have outlined your strategy, defined your processes and systems, and implemented changes, it is vital that you manage the ongoing performance. The key to this is monitoring, measuring, and reporting on the systems and their effectiveness. This data can help you identify areas for improvement and make necessary adjustments to your plan.

1. Monitor your systems and processes
   Once you have documented your systems and processes, monitor them to make sure that they are working effectively. This includes tracking metrics such as customer satisfaction, lead generation, and sales.

2. Know what results your system should produce
   As Gino Wickman, author of *What the Heck Is EOS?: A Complete Guide for Employees in Companies Running on EOS* (Entrepreneurial Operating System), points out, "If you have 50 people doing everything 50 different ways, the increased complexity leads to mass chaos." If you have predictable systems, you will get predictable results.

3. Measure improvement initiatives
   If you find that your systems and processes are not working effectively, you need to measure improvement initiatives. This will help you to identify areas where you can improve and make necessary adjustments.

Here are some additional tips for managing systems and processes in a small business:

- Use a project management tool to help you track your progress
- Get input from your team members when you are designing your systems and processes
- Be flexible and willing to make changes as needed
- Use technology to automate your processes whenever possible

By following these tips, you will ensure that your small business has efficient and effective systems and processes in place. This will help to improve your productivity, reduce costs, and increase customer satisfaction. Here are some specific ways to monitor systems and measure improvement initiatives:

- Set goals and track metrics

    What are your goals for your business?

    Once you know what you want to achieve, track the metrics to measure your progress. For example, if your goal is to increase customer satisfaction, you could track metrics such as customer survey scores and the number of customer complaints.

- Use surveys and feedback forms

    Ask your customers and employees for feedback on your systems and processes to help you identify areas for improvement.

- Conduct audits

    Periodically conduct audits of your systems and processes to make sure that they are still working effectively. This will help you to identify any potential problems before they become serious.

By monitoring your systems and measuring improvement initiatives, you can ensure that your business is continually improving. This will help you to stay ahead of the competition and achieve your business goals.

Finally, here are some tips for reporting on systems and processes:

- Keep your reports clear and concise: They should be easy to understand and should highlight the key findings.

- Use visuals to make your reports more engaging: Charts, graphs, and other visuals can help to illustrate your findings and make your reports more persuasive.

- Share your reports with the right people: Your reports should be shared with the people who need to know the information. This could include your team members, management, or investors.

By reporting on your systems and processes, you can keep everyone informed about your progress and ensure that everyone is on the same page. This will help to improve communication and collaboration within your business.

LEADING YOUR COMPANY TONE IN A CULTURE OF CONTINUOUS IMPROVEMENT

In addition to the systems and processes we have discussed, it is important to create a culture of continuous improvement within your organization. This means encouraging your employees to identify and suggest improvements to your product or service delivery processes.

While making such a request may seem simple, the environment you create can either quash the motivation to be forthcoming or inspire participation. By developing behaviors that encourage the creation of a culture of continuous improvement, you can continually improve your services and deliver a better experience to your customers.

In their recommendations for a company to be successful at continuous improvement, many industry experts agree on one over-riding factor: the culture starts at the top and reflects the leader of the company.

Simon Sinek, best-selling author and speaker, popularized the concept of *Start With Why*, which means finding the purpose behind any action or organization. He has identified empathy as the most important instrument in a leader's toolbox. Sinek tells us that empathy allows a leader to recognize and share other people's feelings, and to inspire those people to take action.

Empathy is based on biology as humans are social animals who need to feel safe and trust each other in order to cooperate and survive. According to Sinek, companies do best when establishing a model of leadership of "Leaders Eat Last" in which leaders put the needs of their followers before their own and create a culture of mutual support and accountability. This kind of leadership fosters innovation, loyalty, and performance, as people are more willing to take risks, share ideas, and work hard when they feel valued and respected.

The opposite of empathy is stress, which triggers a survival mode that makes people selfish, fearful, and short-sighted. Sinek challenges leaders to overcome the pressures of the modern world—competition, technology, and globalization—and to create environments where people can thrive and contribute to a greater cause.

The key is for the head of the company to set the tone and lead by example. To demonstrate a commitment to continuous improvement in their own work and in the way they interact with others. Leaders should be open and willing to make changes based on what they learn.

Communication with the team is vital. Employees are often the best source of ideas for improvement so leaders should regularly ask for improvement ideas from employees and embrace their suggestions. This shows employees that their ideas are valued and that their input is important.

During this process, communicate the benefits of continuous improvement to employees and keep them updated on the progress of improvement initiatives. This can be done through regular meetings, newsletters, or other communication channels. It's also important to celebrate successes and to recognize employees who contribute to continuous improvement.

Employees should also feel empowered to make changes and to take ownership of their work. This can be done by providing employees with the training and resources they need to make changes, and by creating a supportive environment where employees feel comfortable taking risks.

These ideas do not need to be huge, sweeping "boil the ocean" changes. For the team, everyone making small, incremental improvements that add up over time can be hugely efficient and effective. Leaders should emphasize the importance of small, incremental improvements and celebrate even the smallest successes. This aids in inspiring a culture where employees are constantly looking for ways to improve their work.

Here are four primary programs a leader can institute to give structure to the continuous improvement initiative:

- Establish a continuous improvement team
- Create a continuous improvement process
- Provide continuous improvement training modules
- Put a continuous improvement effort reward and recognition program in place.

EFFECTIVELY DOCUMENT OPERATIONAL SYSTEMS AND PROCESSES

We have mentioned documentation several times in the strategic, implementation, and improvement processes. Documentation should be a required activity in your operational systems. In today's rapidly changing business environment, it is more important than ever to have a well-documented understanding of how your company operates as this documentation can help your company quickly and effectively adapt to change.

Well-documented processes and systems help the company scale more easily. When your company grows, it is important to be able to replicate the existing processes and systems in a consistent and efficient manner. This can protect you with employee attrition, for example. When one employee leaves, the replacement can quickly be brought up to speed by following the documentation. And when you reach your endgame, documentation makes the company more attractive for acquisition as the purchase will be fortified by the fact that the new owners will gain intellectual property that increases the company's value.

Speaking of intellectual property, well-documented processes and systems can help the company to protect that asset. By documenting the company's processes and systems, it can be more difficult for competitors to copy them. Other benefits to having your processes and systems well-documented include:

- Increased Consistency and Efficiency
  When processes are documented, everyone involved knows exactly what is expected of them. This helps to ensure that tasks are performed consistently and efficiently, which can lead to improved productivity and reduced errors.

- Improved Training and Onboarding
  New employees can quickly learn the ropes when there is clear and concise process documentation. This can help to reduce the time and resources required for training, and to ensure that new employees are up to speed on the company's processes and systems from day one.

- Better Decision-Making
  When managers have access to clear and concise process documentation, they are better equipped to make informed decisions. This is because they have a better understanding of how the processes work and how changes to the processes could impact the business.

- Reduced Risk of Compliance Violations
  When processes are documented, it is easier to identify and mitigate compliance risks because the documentation can be used to identify areas where the company is not in compliance with regulations.

- Improved Communication and Collaboration
  When processes are documented, it is easier for people to communicate and collaborate effectively because everyone has access to the same information, which can help to avoid misunderstandings and delays.

- Improve Customer Satisfaction
  When processes are well-documented, customers are more likely to have a positive experience because they can be confident that their requests will be handled in a timely and efficient manner.

- Increased Innovation
  When processes are documented, it is easier to identify areas where

the company can improve because the documentation can be used to identify areas where the processes are inefficient or outdated.

- Reduced Costs
Well-documented processes and systems can help to reduce costs in a number of ways. For example, they can help to reduce the number of errors, which can save money on rework. They can also help to improve efficiency, which can save money on time and resources.

HOW TO ESTABLISH A DOCUMENTATION PROCESS

Every business owner needs to understand some key requirements in establishing a documentation process. It takes time and effort to create and maintain good documentation, but it's an investment and a valuable asset of your company that will pay off in the long run.

Documentation is an ongoing process that needs to be maintained and updated regularly as it can be used to train new employees, onboard customers, and communicate with partners. It is a tool with an array of values.

Here are some best practices for your documentation process:

- Start with the end in mind

    What are you hoping to achieve by documenting your processes? Do you want to improve efficiency, compliance, or knowledge transfer? Once you know your goals, you can start to tailor your documentation accordingly.

- Keep it simple and concise

    Your documentation should be easy to understand and follow. Use clear language and avoid jargon. If possible, use visuals to help explain complex concepts.

- Be specific

    Don't just say, "Do this task." Instead, explain exactly what needs to be done, in what order, and by whom. This will help ensure that your processes are followed consistently.

- Keep your documentation up-to-date

    As your processes change, so should your documentation. Make sure to update your documentation regularly so that it always reflects the current state of your business.

- Make your documentation accessible

    Store your documentation in a central location where it can be easily found and accessed by everyone who needs it.

IMPLEMENTING THE DOCUMENTATION PROCEDURE

While keeping best practices in mind, here is a step-by-step guide for you to create documentation to help your business run efficiently and effectively. As mentioned in your continuous improvement thought process, start small. Do not try to document everything at once; rather, start with the most important processes and increase the scope as you go. Communication with stakeholders is key, and the company culture we discussed enhances your ability to do this. Make sure your documentation is completed in a consistent format, and the more visuals it can represent, the better.

Here are the suggested steps for a successful documentation implementation:

1. Identify the processes that need to be documented

    Not all processes need to be documented, so it's important to identify the ones that are most important. Consider the following factors when making your decision:

    - The complexity of the process
    - The number of people who need to know how to do the process
    - The risk of errors if the process is not documented
    - The regulatory requirements for your industry

2. Create a documentation plan

    This plan should include the following:

    - The scope of the documentation project
    - The timeline for completing the project
    - The resources that will be needed
    - The process for approving and updating the documentation

3. Assign responsibility for documentation

    Someone needs to be responsible for managing the documentation project. This person should be familiar with the processes that need to be documented and have the skills to write clear and concise documentation.

4. <u>Gather information for the documentation</u>

   This information can be gathered from a variety of sources, such as:

   - Interviews with employees who are familiar with the process
   - Existing documentation
   - Observations of the process being performed

5. <u>Write the documentation</u>

   The documentation should be clear, concise, and easy to understand. It should include the following:

   - The purpose of the process
   - The steps involved in the process
   - The required inputs and outputs
   - Any special considerations or limitations

6. <u>Review and approve the documentation</u>

   The documentation should be reviewed by the people who will be using it to ensure it is accurate and complete. Once the documentation is approved, it should be made available to everyone who needs it.

7. <u>Maintain the documentation</u>

   The documentation should be kept up-to-date as the processes change. This can be done by creating a process for updating the documentation and reviewing it on a regular basis.

BEST PRACTICES FOR UPDATING YOUR DOCUMENTATION

As mentioned, your documentation needs to be a living entity with a process to update it. Some ideas and best practices for updating your documentation include:

- <u>Have a documentation plan</u>: This plan should outline the goals of the documentation, the target audience, the timeline, and the process for updating and reviewing the documentation.

- <u>Designate a documentation team</u>: This team should be responsible for creating, updating, and reviewing the documentation. The team should include members from all relevant departments, so that the documentation is accurate and complete.

- <u>Test the documentation</u>: The documentation should be tested to ensure that it is accurate and complete. This testing should be done by users who are representative of the target audience.

- <u>Use a document management system</u>: A document management system can keep your documentation organized and accessible. It can also help to track changes to the documentation and to ensure that everyone is using the most up-to-date version.

- <u>Set up a regular review process</u>: The documentation should be reviewed on a regular basis to ensure that it is accurate, complete, and up-to-date. The review process should include input from all relevant stakeholders.

- <u>Encourage feedback:</u> Employees should be encouraged to provide feedback on the documentation. This feedback can help to identify areas that need improvement and to ensure that the documentation is meeting the needs of the users.

Let's check in with our friend, Explorer Jack who bought the McKinley Logistics Company. The company had been struggling somewhat financially, and he realized it had a reputation for poor customer service.

Jack started by refreshing his management team. He brought them up to speed to become experienced professionals who were committed to Operational Excellence. The newly-invigorated team reorganized the company's operations to improve efficiency and invested in new distribution equipment and technology.

The changes quickly paid off. The company's profits increased, and its customer satisfaction ratings improved. Jack was proud of what had been accomplished, but he knew that he could not rest on his laurels because he wanted to make sure that the company continued to improve. He instituted a culture and process for continuous improvement, encouraged employees to share ideas, while providing training and resources, and rewarded employees for their contributions. In doing this, he created a team of employees who were responsible for identifying and implementing new ways to improve the company's operations. The team met regularly to discuss new ideas, and they were given the resources they needed to implement their ideas.

WHAT EXPERTS SAY ABOUT OPERATIONAL EXCELLENCE AND CONTINUOUS IMPROVEMENT

Here is what renowned experts say about this third *Point of Focus*:

"Excellent firms don't believe in excellence - only in constant improvement and constant change."
—Tom Peters, Author of *In Search of Excellence*

"Quality is everyone's responsibility. If you can't describe what you are doing as a process, you don't know what you're doing. It is not enough to do your best; you must know what to do, and then do your best."
—W. Edwards Deming, American Engineer and Management Consultant

"Innovation is not a big breakthrough invention every time. Innovation is a constant thing. But if you don't have an innovative company [team], coming to work every day to find a better way, you don't have a company [team]. You're getting ready to die on the vine. You're always looking for the next innovation, the next niche, the next product improvement, the next service improvement. But always trying to get better."
—Jack Welch, Former CEO of General Electric

"Quality is the result of a carefully constructed cultural environment. It has to be the fabric of the organization, not part of the fabric."
—Phil Crosby, American Quality Control Expert

"Quality is the result of an intelligent effort, not a chance happening."
—Nassim Nicholas Taleb, Risk Analyst and Mathematician

"Quality is never an accident; it is always the result of high intention, sincere effort, intelligent direction and skillful execution."
—John Ruskin, English Art Critic and Social Thinker

SECTION 4: PEOPLE & TEAM BUILDING, THE BLUE POINT OF FOCUS

"If you hire people just because they can do a job, they'll work for your money. But if you hire people who believe what you believe, they'll work for you with blood and sweat and tears."
—Simon Sinek

The *4th Point of Focus* in your NorthStar Strategic Partners compass is your People & Team Building. It is symbolized by Blue.

Blue has a richness that conveys an association with trust and loyalty. Often used in depictions of images for peace, security, and stability, it is appropriate that this color depicts the bond you should have with employees, partners, and customers.

Blue is also known for being calming, especially because of its association with the sea and sky when each are at their calmest. This also accurately depicts the most productive approach when there are conflicts in relationships between people. Approach with calmness.

Blue also means openness, honesty, and sincerity. Apply these qualities liberally in your relationships for deeper more meaningful outcomes.

Blue is the color of imagination and innovation, which are the contributions you should hope for from your key business support.

PEOPLE RELATIONSHIP DYNAMICS IN A COMPANY

Your people are your company. You can have the greatest marketing in the world but as soon as anyone seeks to interact with your company, the person they come in contact with will be the factor that actually defines you, the person who serves them will define the level of service they will associate with your company, and the care of the person who finalizes with them will inspire their level of satisfaction with you.

Positive relations are vital. Employees with positive relationships with their colleagues are more likely to be happy and engaged in their work, which increases productivity and creates a better bottom line for the company. When they feel like they are part of a team and that their contributions are valued, they are more likely to have high morale, inspiring a more positive work environment and lower turnover rates.

When your employees feel comfortable sharing ideas and collaborating with each other, they are more likely to come up with new and innovative solutions to problems, keeping you ahead of the competition.

Clearly, employees are more likely to want to work for a company that has a positive work environment and strong people relations. You will attract and retain top talent and gain a major competitive advantage.

HOW DOES YOUR COMPANY STACK UP?

Here are five key questions a company should ask itself on whether the relationships of the people within it are healthy for the company:

1. <u>Do employees feel comfortable speaking up and sharing their ideas?</u>
   A healthy workplace is one where employees feel comfortable speaking up and sharing their ideas, even if they are different from the majority. If employees feel like they cannot speak freely, it can lead to resentment and stifle innovation.

2. <u>Do employees feel respected and valued by their colleagues and managers?</u>
   Employees who feel respected and valued are more likely to be engaged and productive. They are also more likely to stay with the company for the long term.

3. <u>Do employees feel like they can trust their colleagues and managers?</u>
   Trust is essential for any healthy relationship, including those in the workplace. When employees trust their colleagues and managers, they are more likely to share information and collaborate effectively.

4. <u>Do employees feel like they are part of a team?</u>
   A sense of belonging is important for employee morale and productivity. When employees feel like they are part of a team, they are more likely to be supportive of each other and work towards common goals.

5. <u>Do employees feel like they are able to balance their work and personal lives?</u>
   A healthy work-life balance is important for employee well-being and productivity. When employees feel like they are able to balance their work and personal lives, they are more likely to be engaged and productive at work.

By asking these questions, you can gain insights into the health of the relationships with and between your employees.

HOW LEADERSHIP CAN BUILD TRUST AND RAPPORT

There are some basic ways that you and the other leaders in your company can build trust and rapport with your employees and partners. The first is to be honest and transparent. Partners will trust you and work with you with integrity. Employees are more likely to trust and respect a manager who is honest and transparent with them. This means being open about the company's goals, challenges, and successes.

Second, be supportive and understanding. This will help partners to be transparent with you. Employees need to feel like their manager is there to support them and help them succeed. This means being understanding when people make mistakes and being willing to offer constructive feedback.

Third is to be approachable. Encourage communications from partners, even with complaints. Employees need to feel like they can approach their manager with any questions or concerns. This means being open to communication and making yourself available to partners and your employees.

As you work towards your optimal people relationship environment, set your goals and objectives to meet the standards of a high functioning business team. Consider these:

THE TEN MOST IMPORTANT QUALITIES OF A HIGH-FUNCTIONING BUSINESS TEAM

Here are the ten most important qualities of a high-functioning team as defined within the *NorthStar Strategic Partners 4 Points of Focus* structure:

1. <u>Clear and aligned purpose</u>
   Everyone on the team understands the vision, purpose, and goals of the team and is focused on achieving them.

2. <u>Clear roles and responsibilities</u>
   Everyone on the team knows what their roles and responsibilities are and how they fit into the overall team structure.

3. <u>Trust and mutual respect</u>
   Team members trust and respect each other, even when they disagree. They are willing to share ideas and collaborate openly.

4. <u>Open and clear communication</u>
   Team members communicate openly and honestly with each other, both verbally and in writing. They are always willing to listen to feedback and constructive criticism.

5. <u>Collaboration and teamwork</u>
   Team members are willing to work together and help each other out, even if they don't have the same skills or experience. They are also willing to share credit for success.

6. <u>Problem-solving and creativity</u>
   Team members are able to identify and solve problems creatively and effectively. They are also willing to take risks and try new things.

7. <u>Continuous learning and improvement</u>
   Team members are always looking for ways to improve their skills and knowledge. They are also willing to share their knowledge with others on the team.

8. <u>Adaptability and flexibility</u>
   Team members are able to adapt to change and new challenges. They are also willing to go the extra mile to get the job done.

9. <u>Leadership and motivation</u>
   Team members are willing to step up and take leadership roles when needed. They are also able to motivate and inspire others on the team.

10. <u>Accountability</u>
    Team members are accountable for their own actions and the actions of the team as a whole. They are also willing to take responsibility for their mistakes.

To achieve maximum success in this *Point of Focus*, these are the qualities you need to see in your teams as a result of your people relations initiatives.

COMMUNICATION STRATEGIES TO BOLSTER EMPLOYEE INTERACTION

As you focus on effective communication with and between your employees, it is important that you put some communication infrastructure in place. How these are used is based on the motivation of the participants (which will likely follow behavior that you and your leadership team model). However, without these, they won't have a good opportunity to communicate at all. Some channels of communication to implement might include:

- <u>Hold regular team meetings</u>

    This is a great way to keep everyone up-to-date on the latest news and developments within the company.

- <u>Create a company intranet or collaboration platform</u>

    Whether this is a web intranet or a platform like Microsoft TEAMS, this can be a great way to share information and resources with employees, and between them.

- <u>Use email and instant messaging</u>

    These are two of the most common ways for employees to communicate with each other.

- <u>Encourage face-to-face communication</u>

    This is often the best way to build trust and rapport between employees.

THE INTERPERSONAL RELATIONSHIPS IN YOUR COMPANY

Each person who shows up to work in your company has a unique personality. Those personalities mix, interact, and form relationships which can make your company powerful or, conversely, make it dysfunctional.

It is, therefore, essential to understand the dynamics of relationships within your company if you want to create a positive and productive work environment. Three foundational factors that can affect relationships in a company are:

1. <u>Your company's culture</u>
   Your company's culture can have a big impact on the way that employees interact with each other. In a culture that values open communication, employees are more likely to feel comfortable sharing ideas and feedback, even if they are different from the majority. In a culture that is more hierarchical, employees may be more hesitant to speak up, especially if they are junior employees.

   - In a culture that values teamwork, employees are more likely to work together to achieve common goals.

   - In a culture that is more individualistic, employees may be more focused on their own work and less likely to help their colleagues.

   - In a culture that values conflict resolution, employees are more likely to address problems head-on and work together to find solutions.

   - In a culture that avoids conflict, employees may be more likely to sweep problems under the rug or let them fester.

   - In a culture that values creativity and innovation, employees are more likely to feel comfortable taking risks and trying new things.

   - In a culture that is more risk-averse, employees may be more hesitant to step outside the box.

2. <u>The personality types of the employees</u>
   Working towards building the strengths of employee personality types can also play a role in how they perform and the relationships they form. Ignoring their personality types can create tension and inefficiencies.

3. <u>The way that the company is structured</u>
   The way that the company is structured can also affect relationships between employees.

   - In a company with a flat hierarchy, employees may be more likely to communicate directly with each other, regardless of their position.

   - In a company with a more traditional hierarchy, employees may be more likely to communicate with their direct supervisor or manager.

   - In a company with a team-based structure, employees may be more likely to collaborate with each other on projects and tasks.

- In a company with a more siloed structure, employees may be more likely to work independently and only collaborate with people in their own department or team.

- In a company with a decentralized decision-making process, employees may be more likely to have input into decisions that affect them.

- In a company with a more centralized decision-making process, employees may be more likely to feel like they have less control over their work.

By achieving positive relationships between employees in your company, you will experience a number of positive impacts on your organizational success. These include:

- Increased productivity: When employees have positive relationships with each other, they are more likely to be happy and engaged in their work. This can lead to increased productivity and a better bottom line for the company.

- Improved morale/low turnover: When employees feel like they are part of a team and that their contributions are valued, they are more likely to have high morale. This can lead to a more positive work environment and lower turnover rates.

- Fostered innovation: When employees feel comfortable sharing ideas and collaborating with each other, they are more likely to come up with new and innovative solutions to problems. This can help the company to stay ahead of the competition.

- Greater ability to attract and retain top talent: Employees are more likely to want to work for a company that has a positive work environment and strong people relations. This can help the company to attract and retain top talent, which can be a major competitive advantage.

HOW TO MAKE "PERSONALITY" WORK FOR YOUR COMPANY

Personality: everyone has one and 69% of employers use personality tests as part of their hiring process. A survey by *CareerBuilder* found that 72% of hiring managers said that a candidate's personality was the *deciding factor* in their interview.

As you strategize on how to manage personalities in your company, you must first be aware of your own personality type and how it might affect your interactions with others. You must also be open-minded and willing to learn about other personality types. By understanding these types, it will give you the ability to be respectful of other people's communication styles and work styles. However, your end objective can be more than just a desire to compromise and find solutions that work for everyone. It is also about finding ways to manage to everyone's strengths and weaknesses and optimize the power of personality in elevating your business.

Through awareness and maximization of your employee personality types, your company will be affected in some key functional areas:

- Communication: Employees with different personality types may have different communication styles.

  For example, an extrovert may be more likely to speak up in meetings and share their ideas, while an introvert may be more likely to listen and take in information before speaking. This can lead to misunderstandings and conflict if employees are not aware of each other's communication styles.

- Collaboration: Employees with different personality types may also have different work styles.

  For example, a *detail-oriented* employee may need more time to complete a task, while a more *creative* employee may be able to come up with ideas quickly. This can lead to frustration if employees are not able to adjust their work styles to accommodate each other.

- Conflict resolution: Employees with different personality types may also have different approaches to conflict resolution.

  For example, an *assertive* employee may be more likely to confront a conflict head-on, while a more *passive* employee may be more likely to avoid conflict altogether. This can lead to problems if employees are not able to find a way to resolve conflict in a constructive way.

- Teamwork: Employees with different personality types can also have different strengths and weaknesses.

  For example, an *outgoing* employee may be good at networking and bringing people together, while a more *introverted* employee may be good at working independently and coming up with creative solutions. This can be beneficial if employees are able to leverage each other's strengths and weaknesses to achieve common goals.

HOW TO IDENTIFY "WHO'S WHO IN THE ZOO?"

The phrase "Who's Who in the Zoo" was popularized by a series of Warner Bros. cartoons from the 1940s. The cartoons, which featured a variety of animals who were represented as different types of people, were a humorous way of exploring the different personalities and roles that people play.

If your company is a "zoo," who is who? And how do you find out?

There are numerous self-assessment programs that can help you and your team determine this. Based on "tests" with no wrong answers, they allow the individual participant to identify themselves, their energies, and preferences.

Two popular methodologies are the DiSC and the Myers-Briggs assessment tools.

The DiSC assessment tool is based on the DiSC model of behavior, which was first proposed in 1928 by William Moulton Marston, a physiological psychologist. Marston's model identified four personality traits:

- Dominance (D)
- Influence (i)
- Steadiness (S)
- Compliance (C)

The first DiSC assessment tool was created in 1956 by Walter V. Clarke, an industrial psychologist. Clarke's assessment, called the Activity Vector Analysis (AVA), was a checklist of adjectives on which people indicated descriptions that were accurate about themselves.

The Myers-Briggs Type Indicator (MBTI) is based on the theory of psychological types developed by Carl Jung in the early 20th century. The MBTI was created by Katharine Cook Briggs and her daughter, Isabel Briggs Myers. In the early 1940s, Briggs and Myers began developing their own personality inventory based on Jung's work. They published the first version of the MBTI in 1943. The MBTI has been revised several times since its initial publication. The most recent revision, Form M, was published in 1998. The MBTI is now one of the most widely used personality tests in the world.

The DiSC profile is a personality assessment tool that measures four key personality dimensions:

1. <u>Dominance (D)</u>: People with high D scores are typically assertive, decisive, and results-oriented. They are often seen as leaders and are good at taking charge.

2. <u>Influence (i)</u>: People with high i scores are typically outgoing, expressive, and persuasive. They are often seen as good communicators and are good at building relationships.

3. <u>Steadiness (S)</u>: People with high S scores are typically calm, patient, and cooperative. They are often seen as reliable and trustworthy.

4. <u>Conscientiousness/Compliance (C)</u>: People with high C scores are typically organized, detail-oriented, and thorough. They are often seen as perfectionists and are good at following rules and procedures.

The Myers-Briggs profile personality assessment tool measures these four key personality dimensions:

1. <u>Introversion (I) vs. Extraversion (E)</u>: People with high I scores are typically more reserved and introspective, while people with high E scores are typically more outgoing and sociable.

2. <u>Sensing (S) vs. Intuition (N)</u>: People with high S scores are typically more focused on the present moment and concrete details, while people with high N scores are typically more focused on the future and abstract ideas.

3. <u>Thinking (T) vs. Feeling (F)</u>: People with high T scores are typically more focused on logic and reason, while people with high F scores are typically more focused on values and emotions.

4. <u>Judging (J) vs. Perceiving (P)</u>: People with high J scores are typically more organized and planned, while people with high P scores are typically more flexible and spontaneous.

By using either tool with your team, you can start a process that can lead to significant results.

Each participant can increase their self-awareness. The tools can help each understand their own personality traits and how they impact their behavior. This can also inspire increased self-acceptance and confidence. It can help people identify their strengths and weaknesses and develop strategies for personal growth and, potentially, a more fulfilling and satisfying life.

The tools will help your people understand the different ways that others communicate and how to communicate more effectively. This can lead to improved relationships and teamwork within your company.

These tools help leaders understand their own personality traits and how they impact their leadership style. Working with the information these tools provide can lead to more effective leadership and improved team performance.

HOW TO PRAISE YOUR EMPLOYEES

Now that you may be getting a grasp on who your people are, the next key area in this Point of Focus is how to treat them when they do well, and when they perform poorly.

Praise and recognition are important for all businesses, but they are especially important for small businesses. When your employees feel appreciated, they are more likely to be happy, engaged, and productive. This can lead to a number of benefits for the business, including increased morale, retention, productivity, customer service, and company culture.

Some specific ideas for praise and recognition of your team might include:

- <u>Give them a public shoutout</u>: This could be in the form of a company-wide email, a mention in a staff meeting, or a post on social media.

- <u>Send them a handwritten note</u>: This is a personal and thoughtful way to show your appreciation.

- <u>Give them a small gift</u>: This could be anything from a gift card to a coffee mug with their name on it.

- <u>Nominate them for an award</u>: This could be an internal award, such as employee of the month, or an external award, such as a local business award.

- <u>Give them more responsibility</u>: This shows that you trust and value their work.

- <u>Let them take on a special project</u>: This gives them a chance to showcase their skills and talents.

- <u>Take them out to lunch</u>: This is a great way to get to know them better and show your appreciation.

- <u>Give them a promotion</u>: This is the ultimate show of appreciation.

Probably the best way to institutionalize your intentions to make praise and recognition part of your company culture is to implement a reward system. As you design and evaluate your reward system, there are several critical success factors to incorporate. Get your employees' input. They are absolutely the best to define what will be valued and motivating. Keep the system simple. Make your system flexible. If something is not working, you want to be able to make a quick and easy fix.

Here are the steps to take in setting up your rewards system:

- <u>Define your goals</u>
  What do you hope to achieve with your reward system? Do you want to improve employee morale, retention, productivity, or something else? Once you know your goals, you can start to develop a system that will help you achieve them.

- <u>Identify your target audience</u>
  Who are you rewarding? All employees? Certain departments? Specific employees? Once you know who you are targeting, you can tailor your rewards accordingly.

- <u>Choose the right rewards</u>
  There are many different types of rewards you can offer, such as:

    o Financial rewards: this could include bonuses, raises, or commissions.

    o Non-financial rewards: this could include gift cards, vacation days, or public recognition.

    o Intrinsic rewards: this could include opportunities for growth and development, or a sense of accomplishment.

- Set clear expectations
  Employees need to know what they need to do in order to earn rewards. Make sure your expectations are clear and measurable.

- Be consistent
  Once you have implemented your reward system, it is important to be consistent with it. Reward employees who meet your expectations, and do not reward employees who don't.

- Evaluate your results
  After you have implemented your reward system for a period of time, take some time to evaluate its effectiveness. Are you achieving your goals? Are employees motivated by the rewards? If not, you may need to make some adjustments.

How to Praise

Praise can be a less formal, but absolutely vital, aspect of the recognition process. In offering praise to your employees, here are some significant guidelines to follow:

- Be specific: Tell the employee what they did specifically that you appreciated.

- Be timely: Praise the employee as soon as possible after they do something well.

- Be sincere: The employee should be able to tell that you are genuinely appreciative of their work.

- Be personal: Refer to the employee by name and make eye contact.

- Be positive: Focus on the employee's positive actions, not their negative ones.

- Be brief: Making statements that are to the point are effective. Even good points make the communication irritating if they are discussed at length.

HOW TO REPRIMAND YOUR EMPLOYEES

According to a study by the *Society for Human Resource Management*, the average employee receives a reprimand once every 2.5 years. This number can vary significantly depending on the industry, with employees in customer service and sales roles being more likely to receive reprimands than those in other industries. It is important to note that reprimands should not be used as a regular form of discipline. Instead, they should be reserved for serious offenses or for repeated instances of minor infractions. When reprimanding an employee, it is important to be clear and specific about the behavior that is unacceptable, and to provide the employee with an opportunity to correct their behavior. If the behavior does not improve, then more serious disciplinary action may be necessary.

Giving negative feedback to an employee can be one of the greatest challenges for a leader or manager. Here are some suggested best practices to deploy when you find yourself in that situation:

- <u>Start by praising the employee's strengths</u>: This will help them feel more receptive to the feedback you are about to give.

- <u>Use "I" statements</u>: Instead of saying, "You're always late!" say, "I'm concerned about your tardiness." This shows that the feedback is coming from you, not from a general observation.

- <u>Be open to feedback yourself</u>: Ask the employee how they think they are doing and what they think they could improve on. This shows that you are interested in their perspective and that you're willing to work with them to find solutions.

- <u>Choose the right time and place</u>: Don't give negative feedback in front of others or when the employee is feeling stressed or overwhelmed. Instead, choose a private setting where you can have a calm and productive conversation.

- <u>Be specific and objective</u>: Don't just say, "You're doing a bad job." Instead, be specific about what the employee is doing wrong and how it is affecting their work. For example, instead of saying, "You're not meeting deadlines," you could say, "You missed your deadline for the quarterly report by two weeks, which caused us to miss our sales target."

- <u>Focus on the behavior, not the person</u>: It is important to remember that negative feedback is about the employee's behavior, not their personality. Avoid making personal attacks or using accusatory language. Instead, focus on the specific behavior that you want the employee to change.

- <u>Be respectful and empathetic</u>: Even though you are giving negative feedback, it is important to be respectful and empathetic to the employee. Remember that they may be feeling defensive or embarrassed, so it is important to be patient and understanding.

- <u>Offer constructive suggestions</u>: Don't just tell the employee what they are doing wrong. Instead, offer them constructive suggestions for how they can improve.

    For example, you could say, "I noticed that you missed your deadline for our project. In the future, I would recommend setting up a project plan and breaking the process down into smaller, more manageable tasks."

- <u>End the conversation on a positive note</u>: Reassure the employee that you believe in their ability to improve and that you are there to support them.

- <u>Follow up</u>: After you have given the employee negative feedback, it is important to follow up to see if they've made any changes. If they have not, you may need to have another conversation with them or take further disciplinary action.

MOTIVATIONAL STRATEGIES TO USE TO ATTRACT GREAT TEAM MEMBERS AND RETAIN THEM

Motivating prospective or existing employees is not just to boost up a happy environment, it is a crucial financial strategy. According to a survey by the *Society for Human Resource Management*, the average cost per hire in the United States is $4,700. This includes the costs of advertising the position, sourcing candidates, conducting interviews, and making a job offer. The cost of turnover from losing an employee is even more complex and costly. A study by the *Aberdeen Group* found that the average cost of turnover is 150% of an employee's annual salary. This means that if an employee earns $50,000 per year, the company will spend an average of $75,000 to replace them.

Here are some basics regarding what motivates your current employees and are areas of interest to new prospects who might join your team:

- <u>Salary and benefits</u>

    While money is not the only thing that motivates employees, it is certainly important. Employees want to feel that they are being compensated fairly for their work, and they also want to have access to good benefits, such as health insurance, retirement plans, and paid time off.

- <u>Challenging and meaningful work</u>: Employees want to feel like their work is important and that they are making a difference. They also want to be challenged and to have opportunities to learn and grow.

- <u>Opportunities for advancement</u>: Employees want to feel like they have a future with their company and that they have the opportunity to advance their careers. This could mean being promoted, taking on new responsibilities, or simply being given more opportunities to learn and grow.

- <u>Positive work environment</u>: Employees want to work in a positive and supportive environment where they feel appreciated and respected. They also want to have a good relationship with their co-workers and supervisors.

- <u>Work-life balance</u>: Employees want to be able to balance their work and personal lives. They want to have enough time to spend with their families and friends, and they also want to have time for hobbies and other interests.

It is important to note that what motivates one prospect or employee may not motivate another. Some may be more motivated by money, while others may be more motivated by challenging work or opportunities for advancement. It is important to understand what motivates the individuals you are dealing with and to tailor your motivational efforts accordingly.

Some key pointers to follow to help attract the talent you want might include:

- <u>Make sure the job description is accurate and up-to-date</u>
  This will help to attract the right candidates and reduce the number of unqualified applicants.

- <u>Use effective recruitment methods</u>
  This could include using online job boards, social media, or employee referrals.

- <u>Conduct thorough interviews</u>
  This will help to ensure that the company is hiring the right person for the job.

- <u>Provide good onboarding and training programs</u>
  This will help new employees to get up to speed quickly and become productive members of the team.

WHAT EXPERTS SAY ABOUT THE VALUE OF YOUR PEOPLE TO YOUR ORGANIZATION

Experts generally recognize that a business' people are instrumental to its success.

"A company's employees are its greatest asset and your people are your product."
–Sir Richard Branson

"Leadership is not about being in charge. Leadership is about taking care of those in your charge."
–Simon Sinek, on X (formerly Twitter)

"People who feel good about themselves produce good results."
–Ken Blanchard, Author of *The One Minute Manager*

"If you want something to happen, you have to make people able and you have to make them want to."
–Dr. Steve Kerr, former Chief Learning Officer of General Electric and Goldman Sachs

"Everyone has an invisible sign hanging from their neck saying, 'Make me feel important.'"
–Mary Kay Ash, founder of Mary Kay Cosmetics

"The greatest contribution of a leader is to make others leaders."
– Simon Sinek

"The only sustainable competitive advantage is an organization's ability to learn faster than its competitors."
–Peter Senge, Author of *The Fifth Discipline*

EXPLORER JACK AND HIS DISTRIBUTION COMPANY

Explorer Jack did not stop using his 4 Points of Focus compass when he thought about his people within the company he acquired when he got back to the States. Always a "people person," this had become even more consolidated when he put his life into the hands of his team during their explorations in the jungles of Africa.

He knew that the success of his trucking and distribution company depended on the hard work and dedication of his employees. So, from the day he bought McKinley Family Logistics, he made it a priority to create a positive and supportive work environment, giving his employees special attention. Jack knew their names, their families, and their hobbies, made sure to praise them when they did a good job, and was always there to offer support when they needed it.

To create an inspiring work environment, he decorated the distribution centers with motivational posters and quotes, held regular team-building exercises, and encouraged his employees to share their ideas. He wanted his employees to feel like they were part of something special, and to be excited to come to work every day.

As part of the initiative to create a positive work environment, Jack also created a motivational rewards process where he awarded bonuses to employees who met or exceeded their goals. He also gave out prizes for "Employee of the Month" and "Employee of the Year."

Jack believed in work-life balance; he knew his employees had personal lives outside of work and wanted to make sure that they had time to enjoy them. To do this, he offered flexible work hours and paid vacation days. He also encouraged his employees to take breaks throughout the day and to step away from their work if they needed to.

Finally, Jack gave his employees chances for advancement. He promoted employees who were hard workers and who showed potential for leadership, and created a mentorship program where experienced employees and truckers could mentor new employees. This helped to create a sense of growth and opportunity for all his employees.

As a result of Jack's commitment to his employees, McKinley Family Logistics became a hugely popular company with its customers. They appreciated the company's dedication to customer service and its commitment to getting the job done right. They also appreciated the company's employees, who were friendly, helpful, and knowledgeable.

McKinley Family Logistics won several awards for customer service and employee satisfaction. Jack felt proud of what he had accomplished, but he knew that the employees were the heart and soul of his company and were a significant part of its overall value.

SECTION 5: THE NORTH STAR, POLARIS, AND THE EXIT STRATEGY

If the *4 Points of Focus* make up your business story, the exit strategy—reaching your "North Star," your Polaris—is the writing of your happy ending.

Your exit strategy is the plan for how you will sell your ownership in your company. It is important to have an exit strategy in place, no matter what stage of business you are in. From the day you start, you need to know how you plan to end.

Having this strategy will help you as you seek to maximize your profits, limit your losses, and control the future of your business. If you have a plan, you can make decisions around questions that impact these three areas in context of your end goals. For the business community, having this strategy shows you are a serious business owner who thinks of the future. It helps you attract investors and stakeholders who will gain confidence because you have a plan. It gives you objectives to keep in mind as you tackle challenges and unforeseen issues.

Common exit strategies can include:

- <u>Initial public offering (IPO)</u>: This is when a company sells shares of its stock to the public for the first time.

- <u>Merger or acquisition</u>: This is when another person or company buys your company, or two or more companies combine to form a new company.

- <u>Employee buyout</u>: This is when the employee team of a company buys the company from you and your shareholders.

- Succession: The unexpected happens. A plan needs to be in place should the leader pass away unexpectedly. What will happen to the ownership of the company? For partnerships and small business corporations, there should be a life insurance policy in a buy/sell agreement.

- Liquidation: This is when your company sells all its assets and ceases to exist.

If you have made it this far in implementing the *4 Points of Focus* in the NorthStar Strategic Partners process, your company should be in an excellent position for acquisition due to your resulting value.

In the following, we will explore how each of the *4 Points of Focus* contributed to your overall value and attractiveness to prospective buyers.

YOUR MARKETING STRATEGIES VALUE

Having well executed the first *Point of Focus*—Marketing Strategies—you will have increased your attractiveness for acquisition in these eight key ways:

1. Higher valuation
   A strong brand is often seen as being more valuable than a weak brand. This is because it is associated with positive aspects such as quality, reliability, and trust. As a result, potential buyers may be willing to pay more for a company with a strong brand.

2. Increased customer recognition
   A strong brand is one that is well-known and respected by its customers. This means that your existing customers are loyal, will be more likely to be aware of your company and its products or services, and are primed to do repeat business.

3. Attract buyers of your company
   A strong brand can attract more stakeholders interested in buying the company because it is known as being more desirable. It is already associated with positive aspects such as quality, reliability, and trust. As a result, potential buyers may be more likely to consider buying your company.

4. Your products or services are likely to gain new customers
   A strong brand can make it easier to sell to new customers because it is already familiar to them. This is because they are more likely to be aware of your company and its products or services, and they may already have a positive opinion of your brand.

5. Reduced marketing costs
   A strong brand can reduce marketing costs because the new buyers will not need to spend as much money on advertising and promotion. Potential customers are already aware of your company and its products or services, and they may already be interested in buying from you.

6. Growth potential
   The potential for significant growth is often attractive to acquirers because acquirers can benefit from the growth, which can lead to increased profits and market share.

7. Market share
   A large market share in their industry is attractive because acquirers can benefit from the acquired company's existing customer base and brand recognition.

8. Complementary products or services
   The acquiring company may be seeking complementary products or services to those it already offers. Their hope is to benefit from the combined sales and marketing efforts of the two companies.

YOUR FINANCIAL STRUCTURE & GROWTH VALUE

Having well executed the second *Point of Focus*—Financial Structure & Growth—you will have improved your attractiveness for acquisition in these five key ways:

1. Higher valuation
   A strong Financial Structure & Growth tracking can lead to a higher valuation for your company because it shows that your company is profitable and has the potential to grow in the future. Profitable companies are very attractive to acquirers because the acquirer can see a clear path to financial returns from the acquisition.

2. Increased buyer confidence
   Potential buyers will be more confident in your company if you have strong Financial Structure & Growth tracking in place because it shows that you are a responsible business owner, aware of your company's financial performance.

3. Quicker sales process
   The selling process can be quicker if you have a strong Financial Structure & Growth tracking in place because potential buyers will be able to quickly assess your company's financial performance and make an informed decision about whether to buy.

4. Increased negotiating power
   Having a strong Financial Structure & Growth tracking can give you increased negotiating power with potential buyers because you will be able to provide them with accurate and up-to-date information about your company's financial performance, which will give you a stronger bargaining position.

5. Reduced risk
   A strong Financial Structure & Growth tracking can reduce the risk for potential buyers because it shows that your company is financially stable and has a track record of success.

YOUR OPERATIONAL EXCELLENCE VALUE

Having well executed the third *Point of Focus*—Operational Excellence—you will have elevated your attractiveness for acquisition in these seven key ways:

1. Higher valuation
   A strong infrastructure and a culture of continuous improvement can lead to a higher valuation for your company because it shows that your company is well-run and has the potential to continue to grow and improve in the future.

2. Increased buyer confidence
   Potential buyers will be more confident in your company if you have a strong infrastructure and a culture of continuous improvement because it shows that you are a responsible business owner who is committed to running a smooth and efficient operation.

3. <u>Quicker sales process</u>
   The selling process can be quicker if you have a strong infrastructure and a culture of continuous improvement in place because potential buyers will be able to quickly assess your company's operations and make an informed decision about whether to buy.

4. <u>Increased negotiating power</u>
   Having a strong infrastructure and a culture of continuous improvement can give you increased negotiating power with potential buyers because you will be able to provide them with evidence of your company's operational excellence, which will give you a stronger bargaining position.

5. <u>Reduced risk</u>
   A strong infrastructure and a culture of continuous improvement can reduce the risk for potential buyers because it shows that your company is well-run and has a track record of success.

6. <u>Technology</u>
   True Operational Excellence means that you have invested in cutting-edge technology which is attractive to acquirers. They will want to benefit from your company's technology and intellectual property.

7. <u>Regulatory approvals</u>
   Your Operational Excellence process should have you on top of all regulatory requirements. The ease of obtaining regulatory approvals would otherwise be a factor in determining whether your company is attractive for acquisition. Some industries, such as healthcare and telecommunications, require extensive regulatory approvals, which can make acquisitions more difficult and time-consuming if they are not in place.

YOUR PEOPLE & TEAM BUILDING VALUE

Having well executed the fourth *Point of Focus*—People & Team Building—you will have heightened your attractiveness for acquisition in these six key ways:

1. Higher valuation
   A strong positive work culture can lead to a higher valuation for your company because it shows that your company is a good place to work, which leads to lower turnover and increased productivity.

2. Increased buyer confidence
   Potential buyers will be more confident in your company if you have a strong positive work culture, which shows that you are a responsible business owner who cares about your employees and partners.

3. Quicker sales process
   The selling process can be quicker if you have a strong positive work culture in place because potential buyers will be able to quickly assess your company's culture, which leads to making an informed decision to buy.

4. Increased negotiating power
   Having a strong positive work culture can give you increased negotiating power with potential buyers because you will be able to provide them with a team they could not accumulate otherwise.

5. Reduced risk
   A strong positive work culture can reduce the risk for potential buyers because it promises staff cohesiveness, with talent wanting to stay together post-acquisition.

6. Management team
   The quality of your management team is also an important factor in determining whether your company is attractive for acquisition. Acquirers may want to be sure that the acquired company has a strong management team who can continue to run the business successfully after the acquisition.

VALUATION METHODS TO DETERMINE THE WORTH OF YOUR COMPANY AND WHEN TO SELL IT

When ready, and after knowing that your *4 Points of Focus* have each reached an impressive level, it is time to ask the basic question: What is my company worth?

Ultimately, the best way to determine the specific value of your company is to consult with a qualified business valuation professional. They will help you choose the right method for your company and its specific circumstances.

There are many different methods that can be used to value a company. Some of the most common methods include:

- Market capitalization
  This is the simplest method and is calculated by multiplying the company's share price by its total number of shares outstanding. Market capitalization is a good method to use if you want to get a quick estimate of a company's value. However, it does not apply if the company's stock is not public and actively traded.

- Book value
  This is the value of a company's assets minus its liabilities. Book value is a good method to use if you want to get a conservative estimate of a company's value. However, it may not be accurate if the company has significant intangible assets, such as brand value or goodwill.

- Discounted cash flow (DCF)
  This method estimates the present value of a company's future cash flows. DCF is a more complex method, but it can be more accurate than the other methods, if done correctly. However, it can be time-consuming and requires making assumptions about the company's future cash flow.

- Precedent transactions
  This method looks at the prices paid for similar companies that have been acquired in recent transactions. Precedent transactions are a good method to use if there have been recent acquisitions of similar companies. However, it can be difficult to find comparable transactions, and the prices paid may not be relevant to your company.

Once you have determined the worth of your company, there are a few indicators that suggest that the market is strong for mergers and acquisitions, and that this is the right time to sell. Indicators to watch include:

- High levels of corporate cash: Companies are sitting on record levels of cash that they may be looking to invest in new businesses or to acquire existing businesses.

- Low interest rates: Low interest rates make it more affordable for companies to borrow money to finance acquisitions.

- Strong economic growth: A strong economy is often accompanied by increased M&A activity, as companies look to expand their businesses or to acquire new markets.

If these indicators are present, it may be a good time for you to consider selling your company. There is no guarantee that a company will sell for a good price, even in a strong market, so lean heavily on professional advice before selling your business.

NorthStar Strategic Partners can help you assess when it is the right time to sell and assist in determining the value of your business.

UNDERSTANDING THE DIFFERENT TYPES OF BUYERS

Selling a company can be a complex process, but it can also be a rewarding one. By understanding the different types of buyers and positioning yourself strategically, you can increase your chances of selling your company for a good price and on your terms.

Before you start marketing your company, identify the different types of buyers in your market and target your marketing efforts to find the right buyer for your business. Potential buyers will be likely to have a lot of questions about your business. Be prepared for the priorities pertinent to the buyer type so you can answer the questions specifically, honestly, and in detail.

Here are four of the key types of buyers you might target:

1. Strategic buyers
   These companies are looking to acquire your business to expand their operations or enter new markets. They are typically interested in businesses similar to their own in terms of size, industry, and target market. Strategic buyers are typically willing to pay the most

for your business, but they may also be more demanding regarding the terms of the sale.

2. <u>Financial buyers</u>
   These companies are looking to acquire your business as an investment. They typically have a lot of capital and are looking to buy businesses that they can grow and sell for a profit in a few years. Financial buyers are typically less willing to pay as much for your business, but they may be more flexible regarding the terms of the sale.

3. <u>Individual buyers</u>
   These people are looking to buy a business to own and operate themselves. They may wish to start their own business or retire from their current job and own a business.

4. <u>Employee buyers</u>
   These are employees of your company who are looking to buy the business from you. They may be interested in keeping the business running as is or making changes to it.

Individual buyers and employee buyers may be willing to pay less for your business, but they may also be more interested in keeping the business running as is.

PUTTING TOGETHER YOUR BUSINESS SALES TEAM AND PROCESS

There are many essential resources for executing a successful exit strategy. Here are some places you can find these resources:

- <u>Industry publications</u>: Industry publications can provide you with information about the latest trends in your industry and the valuation of similar businesses.

- <u>Online resources</u>: There are a number of online resources, such as websites, blogs, and forums, that can provide you with information about selling a business.

- <u>Networking</u>: Networking with other business owners who have sold their companies can provide you with valuable insights and advice.

Your resource team should include:

- **NorthStar Strategic Partners**
  Again, we can help you with the financial aspects of selling your company, such as preparing financial statements and valuing assets. We can also help you with your personal finances after you sell your company and transition you to a financial advisor.

- **A business valuation expert**
  A business valuation expert can help you determine the value of your company and advise you on the best time to sell. NorthStar Strategic Partners can assist in this step.

- **A mergers and acquisitions (M&A) advisor**
  An M&A advisor can help you prepare your company for sale, market your company, and negotiate the terms of the sale.

- **An attorney**
  An attorney can help you with the legal aspects of selling your company, such as drafting contracts and negotiating terms.

- **CPA/Tax professional**
  It is highly recommended that you do tax planning BEFORE you sell the business. There are different tax strategies that can be explored to see if one of them is a right fit for you. Planning can help you pay your fair share of taxes and enable you to plan for your future. NorthStar Strategic Partners can assist you in evaluating various scenarios and partner with your other team members to find a good solution for you.

By utilizing essential resources, you can increase your chances of executing a successful exit strategy. The earlier you start to plan your exit strategy, the more time you will have to gather the necessary resources and prepare your company for sale. It is important to be realistic about the value of your company and the time it may take to sell. Your buyer, once you find them, will likely have different expectations about the price and terms of the sale, so be prepared to negotiate and compromise to reach an agreement that is mutually beneficial.

Once you have reached an agreement with the buyer, it is important to get everything in writing. This includes the purchase price, payment terms, and any other relevant terms. After you have signed the paperwork, it is important to follow through on your commitments. This includes providing the buyer with all the necessary information and documentation.

WHAT EXPERTS SAY ABOUT EXIT STRATEGIES

Experts offer a range of advice for the small business owner designing an exit strategy. "Focus on your goals" and "Strategize" are two strong common themes.

The *NorthStar Strategic Partners 4 Points of Focus* are key. As you build your company to excel in all *4 Points*, you prepare it for your exit strategy. You should put your exit process in place 12 to 24 months before you want to implement the sale.

Additional thoughts by the experts include:

"A business is not just an asset. It's a collection of relationships, processes, and systems that create value. The best businesses are built to sell. They're designed to be easy to understand, operate, and transfer to a new owner."
–John Warrillow, Author, Founder Value Builder System

"You must stay adaptable when writing and executing your exit strategy. It's better to bend a little than to be so rigid that you end up turning off potential buyers or causing undue tension. Keeping an open mind to all possibilities puts you on a stronger footing and may result in an even better outcome than you initially imagined."
–Amanda Dixon, CEO Barney

"You create an exit strategy as you make a company. You don't wait till you're five years in it. You create an exit strategy as you make a company."
–Nipsey Hussle, Entrepreneur and Rapper

"Your time is limited, so don't waste it living someone else's life. Don't be trapped by dogma—which is living with the results of other people's thinking. Don't let the noise of others' opinions drown out your own inner voice. And most important, have the courage to follow your heart and intuition. They somehow already know what you truly want to become. Everything else is secondary."
–Steve Jobs, Founder of Apple

"The path to success is to take massive, determined action."
—Tony Robbins, Motivational Speaker

"Always start at the end before you begin. Professional investors always have an exit strategy before they invest. Knowing your exit strategy is an important investment fundamental."
—Robert Kiyosaki, Businessman and Author

EPILOGUE

So, what happened to Adventurer Jack?

Jack was all about logistics. If you remember, when he heard that the McKinley Family Logistics Company was up for sale, he jumped at the chance to buy it. The company was a small trucking company with several distribution centers that delivered beverages to local retail and merchants, restaurants, and bars. Jack knew that with some investment and hard work, he could make the company a big success.

Just as he did in his exploration adventures, Jack sat down to map out his plan. He used a special compass this time: NorthStar Strategic Partners 4 Points of Focus. He knew that if he threw all his efforts into these 4 key areas, he would accomplish his goal, which was to build a valuable asset, sell it, and finance his next big exploration.

Jack's first step was to **rebrand the company**. He leveraged the McKinley Family reputation but developed a new logo that was more modern and appealing. Then he created a narrative about the friendliness, efficiency and expertise of the company and built that reputation into the brand story. He also invested in marketing and advertising to raise awareness of the company's services and a new brand narrative.

In addition to rebranding, Jack worked to **improve the company's financial system**. He implemented new accounting software and procedures that more accurately tracked the company's finances. He also created a sound financial plan that outlined the company's goals and how it would achieve them.

Jack prioritized **improving the company's operations**. He invested in new equipment and technology that made the company more efficient. He also implemented a continuous improvement process that was based on his employees' involvement, customer input and partner recommendations which allowed the company to identify and fix problems before they became major issues.

He created a **unified team** across the organization. Every individual felt seen, heard, and recognized. His reward system was very popular, and the team loved vying for its payouts. Praises and reprimands were both received well by employees, which made the team improve steadily.

As a result of Jack's hard work, the McKinley Family Logistics Company quickly became a success. The company's profits increased, its customer base grew, and its employees were happy and motivated.

Meeting his growth and efficiency targets, Jack decided that it was time to sell the company. He knew that the company was in good hands with its talented employees, and he was confident that they would continue to grow and succeed.

Jack approached the company's key employees about buying the company, and they were eager to take on the challenge. They worked with Jack to put together a financing plan, and the sale was finalized a few months later.

Jack was happy to see the company in the hands of people who were passionate about it and who he knew would continue to make it a success. He was also proud of all he had accomplished in the few years since he bought the company; he took a small, mediocre business and turned it into a thriving success.

Using his NorthStar Strategic Partners 4 Points of Focus business compass, Jack's exit strategy was a success. He had created a valuable asset that he was able to sell at a profit. He had also helped to create a successful business that would continue to thrive in the years to come.

Jack packed his bags and headed off to his next dream, to find the legendary Lost City of Z, reputed to be hidden deep in the Amazonian Rain Forest. While the Southern Cross would be his guide in the southern hemisphere, and Polaris would not be, he still had what served him the best:

The 4 Points of Focus™

N✧RTHSTAR
Strategic Partners

WHAT ARE YOUR NEXT STEPS?

Contact NorthStar Strategic Partners for a diagnostic consultation and get started with a coach who will empower you to reach your dreams.

ABOUT THE AUTHOR

WENDY ROBERTS

Wendy Roberts is the visionary and CEO of NorthStar Strategic Partners. The first thing she will tell you is that she is left-handed. Why is this important? Because Wendy will always approach things with out-of-box, solution-oriented, non-cookie-cutter innovation. She leads our company of business consulting firm professionals that way, and will influence yours that way as well. She has a vast record of driving powerful business consulting firm strategies using emerging technologies including data analytics, AI, cybersecurity, and GRC solutions.

As an accomplished global business valuation and finance executive, audit committee member, and business advisor Wendy has over 25+ years experience in financial and audit leadership, operations expertise, and technology innovation for both SMB and multinational companies. As a corporate finance executive, she delivered relevant expertise in corporate strategy, risk management, financial reporting, M&A, IT operations, audit/SOX reporting and system implementations. She has acted as the CFO for various startups including an early-stage software company, successfully selling it to a large publicly traded company. She spent many years in the public accounting area delivering solid results for her customers in accounting, audit, tax and IT systems.

CPA licensed, she has also held the CIA, CISA and CCSA designations and MCSE in IT systems engineering. Wendy is currently serving on the Audit Committee of The Tech Interactive, a world leader in the creation of immersive STEAM education resources to develop the next generation of problem solvers.

ACKNOWLEDGEMENTS

I would like to express my heartfelt gratitude to my right-hand person, Rob Watson, who agreed to join me on this journey. You helped me take this dream of writing a book and making it a reality. I am also deeply thankful to my editor, Ruth Fae, for your invaluable insights and guidance, and to my publisher and book designer, K. LaFleur and Kristina Conatser, for carrying the book over the finish line.

I also want to thank my internal team, Catie Cain and Shy Sayno, for all the support and dedication over the last year.

And, finally, to my readers, thank you for giving this book a purpose.

Wendy

REFERENCES

Books Mentioned:

Blanchard, Ken. *The One Minute Manager* HarperCollins GB; New Thorsons Classics edition (25 May 2015)

Miller, Donald. *How to Grow Your Small Business: A 6-Step Plan to Help Your Business Take Off* HarperCollins Leadership (14 March 2023)

Peters, Tom & Waterman Jnr, Robert H. In Search of Excellence: Lessons from America's Best-Run Companies: *Lessons from America's Best-Run Companies* Profile Trade; 1st edition (27 May 2015)

Senge, Peter. *The Fifth Discipline: The Art & Practice of The Learning Organization Crown*; Illustrated edition (21 March 2006)

Sinek, Simon. *Start With Why: The Inspiring Million-Copy Bestseller That Will Help You Find Your Purpose* Penguin (General UK); 1st edition (7 November 2011)

Wickman, Gino & Bouwer, Tom. *What the Heck Is EOS?: A Complete Guide for Employees in Companies Running on EOS.* BenBella Books (5 September 2017)

People Mentioned:

Ash, Mary Kay: Founder of Mary Kay Cosmetics

Baer, Jay: Author and inspirational Marketing Speaker jaybaer.com

Branson, Sir Richard: Founder of the Virgin Group

Buffett, Warren: Chairman and CEO of Berkshire Hathaway

Crosby, Phil: American Quality Control Expert

Deming, W. Edwards: Engineer and Management Consultant The Deming Institute

Dimon, Jamie: Chairman and CEO of JPMorgan Chase

Dixon, Amanda: CEO of Barney

Godin, Seth: Author and Marketing Guru sethgodin.com

Hussle, Nipsey: Entrepreneur and Rapper

Jobs, Steve: Founder of Apple

Kerr, Dr, Steve: drstevenkerr.com

Kiyosaki, Robert, Businessman and Author richdad.com

Lynch, Peter: Author, Former Investment Manager of Fidelity Magellan Fund

Robbins, Tony: Motivational Speaker tonyrobbins.com

Ruskin, John: English Art Critic and Social Thinker

Taleb, Nassim Nicholas: Author, Risk Analyst and Mathematician

Vaynerchuk, Gary: Entrepreneur, Speaker, and Marketing Expert garyvaynerchuk.com

Warrillow, John: Built To Sell

Welch, Jack: Former CEO of General Electric

Tools Mentioned:

CareerBuilder www.careerbuilder.com

DiSC www.discprofile.com

Myers-Briggs www.themyersbriggs.com

Made in the USA
Columbia, SC
13 February 2024